SILVER™
series

Welcome to
Computer
Basics

MICROSOFT®
WINDOWS® 10
AND OFFICE ONLINE
by Greg Marshall

LABYRINTH
LEARNING™

Berkeley, CA

President:
Brian Favro

Product Manager:
Natalie Zifcak

Development Manager:
Laura Popelka

Production Manager:
Debra Grose

Senior Editor:
Alexandra Mummery

Junior Editor:
Alexandria Henderson

Composition:
Happenstance Type-o-rama

Cover Design:
Mick Koller, SuperLab Design

LABYRINTH
LEARNING™

Welcome to Computer Basics: Microsoft Windows 10 and Office Online
by Greg P. Marshall II

Labyrinth Learning
2560 9th Street, Suite 320
Berkeley, CA 94710
800.522.9746
On the web at lablearning.com

Photo and illustration credits: p. 8, © Creative Commons, Jason Kinch Photographic; p. 9, © afrank99 (own work) via Wikimedia Commons; © Aidan C. Siegel, Aido2002 via Wikimedia Commons; p. 155, © Darkone (own work) via Wikimedia Commons; p. 156, © Harke (own work) via Wikimedia Commons

ITEM: 1-59136-791-3
ISBN-13: 978-159136-791-8

Manufactured in the United States of America

10 9 8 7 6 5 4 3 2 1

Table of Contents

UNIT 1

Windows 10 Basics

CHAPTER 1

Getting Your First Look 3

CHAPTER 2

Starting and Controlling Apps 37

CHAPTER 3

Creating an Online Account 65

UNIT 2

File Management

UNIT 3

The Internet and More

CHAPTER 8

Using the Internet 215

CHAPTER 9

Researching on the Internet. 247

CHAPTER 10

Using Settings and Help. 271

Preface

Why did we write this book? All new PCs come with Windows 10 and the free tools of Office Online. This new environment is quite different from many of the previous Windows versions, and some of the changes can be difficult to get comfortable with! Our goal is to provide educators with a curriculum that meets the needs of a class providing a basic introduction to this new operating system. We hope this material is useful for a short course in a continuing education program, a one-credit class in a college environment, or enhancing skills for adults in a community education class.

What key elements did we factor into our solution? From speaking with instructors who teach this material, we learned that the following elements are critical for effective learning:

- Simplicity

- Ease of reading and comprehension

- Realistic examples that students can relate to the real world

- Lots of graphics and illustrations to reinforce the text discussions

- Hands-on practice that walks students through task completion

What is covered in this book? *Welcome to Computer Basics: Windows 10 and Office Online* is a complete introduction to Microsoft's new operating system and basic computer concepts to ensure students develop the skills they need to effectively use a computer.

In Unit 1, students begin their exploration of Windows 10. We focus on the tools that students will use every day, aiding productivity in school and at work. Features covered include program controls, menus, working with the Start menu (it's back!), using the taskbar, and basic word processing. Students start programs, create an Office Online account, work with apps, and use email.

A critical skill for all computer work is learning how and where to save files, so in Unit 2, students tackle file management. In fact, file management and organization is woven throughout the course, as students save files and create folders both on the local PC and in the cloud.

In Unit 3, students learn best practices for using the Internet. We cover Microsoft's new web browser, Edge, and focus on effective searches and how to protect against Internet threats. We integrate coverage of Outlook Online, Word Online, and OneDrive as well. We also cover how to manage settings and preferences within Windows 10.

Every chapter includes a Concepts Review quiz as well as end-of-chapter exercises (Skill Builder and Try This at Home exercises).

How does our approach work? For more than two decades, Labyrinth Learning has been working to perfect our *unique instructional design*. The benefit of our approach is that learning is faster and easier for students. This book includes elements that will allow for effective learning for a wide range of learning levels and styles. Key features include:

- Concise concept discussions followed by Hands-On exercises that give students experience with those concepts right away

- Figures that are specific to the task and are easily understood

- Quick Reference sections that summarize key tasks with generic steps that will work without repeating an exercise

- Hands-On exercises that contain a large number of illustrated steps to make them easier to follow

- Skill Builder exercises in each chapter, which are less detailed than Hands-On exercises

- Try This at Home exercises, where applicable, that further challenge students by asking them to complete an exercise outside of the classroom

- A Student Resource Center that provides access to chapter quizzes, WebSims and videos, overview presentations, and more helpful information to aid in their study

What instructor resources have we included? This course is supported on the Labyrinth website with a comprehensive instructor support package that includes detailed lesson plans, PowerPoint presentations, a course syllabus, additional Skill Builder exercises, test banks, and more.

Visual Conventions

This book uses many visual and typographical cues to guide you through the chapters. The following table provides examples and describes the functions of each cue.

`Type this text`	Anything you should type on the keyboard is shown like this.
Tip!	Tips, Notes, and Warnings are used throughout the text to draw attention to certain topics.
Command→ **Command→Command**	This convention indicates selections to be made from a Ribbon or menu bar. For example, **File→Save** means to select File and then select Save.
FROM THE KEYBOARD	These notes indicate shortcut keys for executing tasks described in the text.
QUICK REFERENCE:	Quick Reference tables provide generic instructions for key tasks. Only perform these tasks if you are instructed to do so in an exercise.
	This icon indicates the availability of a short video demo of a particular topic. Find the video on the Student Resource Center.
ON THE WEB	This icon indicates the availability of a web-based simulation (WebSim) for an exercise that would otherwise be difficult to set up or would be prohibited in a classroom environment. These are a key advantage for your lab!
HANDS-ON	Hands-On exercises appear immediately after concept discussions, and they provide step-by-step instructions and plenty of illustrations.
	Concepts Review quizzes include true/false and multiple-choice questions designed to gauge your understanding of the material.
	Skill Builder exercises provide additional hands-on practice with moderate assistance.
	Try This at Home exercises allow you to test your skills outside the classroom with special projects and activities.

UNIT 1: WINDOWS 10 BASICS

In this unit, you will start exploring Microsoft's newest operating system, Windows 10. Topics covered in Chapters 1–2 include starting and properly shutting down the computer, logging in, using a mouse, navigating the basic features of the opening screen known as the Desktop, employing touch controls, and switching between apps. Chapter 3 addresses how and why you should create a Microsoft account. Topics covered in Chapters 4 and 5 include how to work with apps, how and where to save your work, using Word Online for typing and editing, how to use email, and email safety.

CHAPTER 1

Getting Your First Look

LEARNING OBJECTIVES

- Log in to the computer using a username and a password
- Describe the basic layout of the Windows 10 Desktop screen
- Use the mouse to right-click and drag
- Work with the Start menu
- Shut down the computer correctly

Windows 10 is the newest version of Microsoft's operating system. With this release, Microsoft continues toward its goal of making access to the functionality of the computer easier and less frustrating for both new and experienced users. In this chapter, you will start the computer, navigate basic features of the opening screen known as the Desktop, use the mouse skills necessary to navigate in Windows, and properly shut down the computer.

Learning Resources: **labyrinthelab.com/wtcb10**

📁 Case Study: Starting Something New

Cherize moved into her son's home. Her son, Patrick, wanted Cherize to have access to the family computer so she could play games such as Solitaire, learn to use email, and search the Internet. To give Cherize privacy, her son set up a separate username and password.

Cherize was scared the first time she sat down at the computer, but Patrick said, "Push the power button and start using it. And don't worry; you won't break anything." Her son explained the log in screen to her and showed her how to enter her password.

When another colorful screen appeared, Patrick said, "That's the Desktop. Here is the Start button that gives you access to all of your programs. Single-click the icons in the Start menu to see the programs you have."

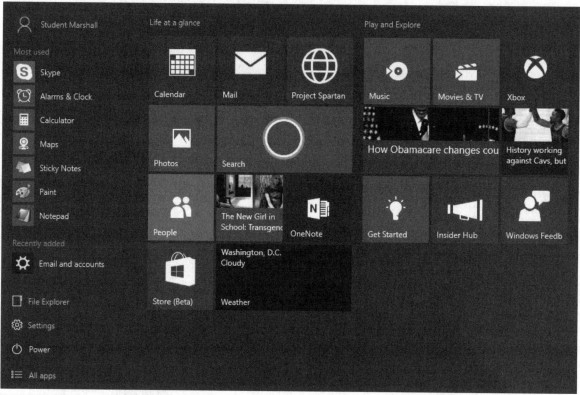

Example of the Start menu screen

At first she had difficulty, but after a while, Cherize became more comfortable with the mouse and rarely had to look at it before clicking. She began to think, "Using this computer is going to be fun."

Logging In to Windows

Most computer systems used in schools and businesses are **networked**, or connected. An important part of keeping a network secure is making sure everyone using computers on the network is authorized to do so. Logging in to the computer is the process of entering your username and password to gain access to the computer and network.

Passwords

A critical piece of the login process is the password. Your password allows you into the computer. Your password must be entered correctly every time. For example *Pa!z4EV* is not the same as *pa!z4ev*.

 Warning! Passwords should never be shared. Sharing passwords is one of the top reasons people have their computer and financial information stolen.

Creating Your Own Passwords

When creating your own password for a home or office computer, don't use familiar names, birthdays, or common words that can be easily guessed. A secure password will contain a mixture of uppercase and lowercase letters, numbers, and punctuation.

The following are some examples of good and poor passwords.

EXAMPLES OF PASSWORDS

Good Passwords	Poor Passwords
!GreeN2	Fido
8Ate8	Johndoe
Fun2Dr1v	12345678
AcEsn8s	Password

What Happens During the Startup Process?

From the moment you turn on the computer and throughout the login process, the computer and Windows are working together to get ready for you. Windows is not one giant program but rather a collection of hundreds of little programs, so as the computer starts, the various parts and pieces of Windows are starting as well. Together they form the **operating system** that we see and work with on the screen.

🖱 HANDS-ON 1.1 Log In to Windows 10

In this exercise, you will log in to your computer using the login name and password provided by your instructor.

1. If necessary, turn on the computer and monitor. (The computer may already be switched on if you are in a computer lab.) Ask your instructor for help if necessary.

After a pause, the computer begins starting up, which usually takes about a minute. When the startup process is complete, the lock screen appears.

2. Click the **lock** screen to bring up the sign-in screen.

The lock screen covers the sign-in screen with a changing image and provides the date and time. If you take too long when entering your login and password, the lock screen will reappear.

3. Click the appropriate login from the bottom-left of the screen. Your login may be the only one listed.

Notice that clicking on a login causes it to show in the middle of the screen. In the following example we have chosen Student Marshall, but you should use your login.

4. Enter the password you were given into the blank password line and click the **arrow** button. This will take you to the Desktop.

The Windows 10 Desktop

Once you have logged in to the computer, you will be looking at the Windows 10 Desktop. The Desktop is the primary work area in Windows 10, and like your desk at school, all the apps you are working with are placed on the Desktop.

The Desktop has many unique features that help you to be more efficient when using the computer.

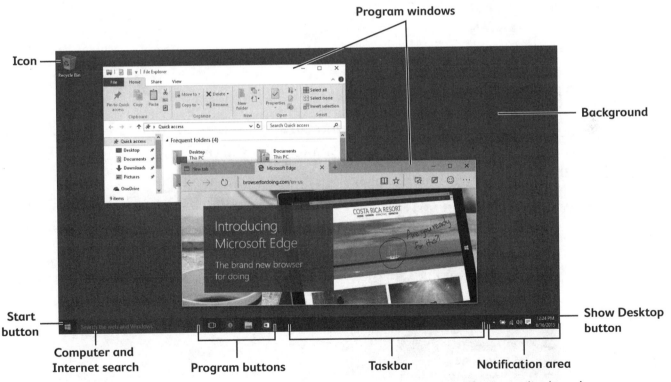

This is what the Windows 10 Desktop looks like with some common features displayed.

Basic Computer Components

Your computer is a collection of hardware parts working together with Windows 10 and other software applications. Knowing the name and function of various components can give you a better understanding of the computing process.

Processor

The processor is often referred to as the "brain" of the computer. The central processing unit (CPU) does all the processing that keeps programs running, moves the cards when you play Solitaire, and does the math in your spreadsheet programs. How quickly these processes are carried out is largely determined by the gigahertz (GHz) rating of the CPU. A larger GHz rating means the processor is capable of significantly more (billions more!) processing cycles per second.

Intel's i7 is a popular processor for computers running Windows 10.

Hard Drive

The **hard drive** is the **permanent storage** device in the computer. You can think of the hard drive as a large filing cabinet where all the files and programs that run on the computer are stored.

A hard drive from Western Digital.

Random Access Memory (RAM)

Hard drives operate at a relatively slow speed, so your computer does not run programs directly from the hard drive. When a program is used, it is first loaded into random access memory (RAM) to take advantage of the very high speed at which it allows data to be accessed by the CPU. As you edit a letter or make a drawing, the information is being stored in RAM. RAM is considered temporary memory, though, because unlike the hard drive, when the computer is turned off, all of the data in RAM is lost.

An example of random access memory for a laptop

Universal Serial Bus (USB)

A universal serial bus (USB) port is a small rectangular port or connector now common on all computers that allows you to connect various pieces of equipment to your computer using a single standardized cord and plug. USB ports come in two basic sizes that both provide the same connection services. Once a device is connected via a USB port, Windows 10 will recognize the equipment and help with its configuration. Before USB, different equipment had special connectors and cables, and it was much more difficult for new users to set up their computers.

A cable you can plug into a USB device

A typical USB port located on the front or side of a computer

Here are examples of a USB plug and port. Notice the universal symbol for USB on both the plug and equipment.

Start Button

The square button in the bottom-left corner of the screen displaying the Windows logo is called the Start button. Access to most of Windows 10's features, your software, and your documents starts from this button in what's called the Start menu. Microsoft wants you to remember that everything "starts" with this little square button.

Icons

Icons are small pictures on the screen that represent programs or other features. You can launch these programs and features by double-clicking on their icons. In the previous illustration, you will notice an icon in the upper-left corner labeled Recycle Bin. This represents the Recycle Bin folder, where files are moved when deleted (as discussed later in this book).

Typical Windows 10 icons

Notification Area

The notification area is located on the taskbar in the bottom-right corner of the computer screen. The notification area contains icons for programs that are currently running but don't necessarily need a lot of user interaction, such as antivirus programs, Internet connection software, Microsoft Outlook email, and possibly the software that allows your computer to communicate with your printer.

If you use your mouse pointer to hover over an icon in the Notification Area, a small ScreenTip will appear that tells you what that program does or is doing. ScreenTips are helpful if you're curious about what's going on in your computer.

Network Connection

Most computers will be connected to the Internet and, in a school or business environment, to a local network. This connection can be made either by using a network cable that plugs into the network port on your computer or by using the radio transmitter in your computer to connect wirelessly.

Besides providing you access to the Internet, the network connection at school or work may also give you access to printers and shared documents.

Using a Mouse

The mouse is your main tool for controlling programs on the Windows 10 Desktop. Moving the mouse with your hand controls the movements of the **mouse pointer** on the screen. With your mouse on a flat surface (a table or mouse pad), place your hand on the mouse as shown below so your index finger rests lightly on or above the left mouse button. You may find that dragging your thumb on the flat surface next to the mouse as you move and click can help you control the movement of the mouse.

When you hold the mouse, your index finger should rest lightly on the left button.

Note! Keep your wrist straight when using the mouse. The top of the mouse should point toward the top of the mouse pad or workspace. Don't steer the mouse like a car, as twisting/turning it disorients the mouse pointer.

Mouse Motions

There are five basic actions that you can take with the mouse: point, click, drag, double-click, and right-click. With an understanding of these basic actions, you can use the mouse to control most features in Windows 10.

MOUSE MOTIONS

Motion	Notes and How to Do It
Point	<ul><li>Used to view ScreenTips or highlight icons and buttons before selecting.</li><li>Hold the tip of the mouse pointer over an element on the screen.</li><li>Keep the mouse steady.</li><li>Only the tip of the mouse pointer is active.</li></ul>
Click (single-click)	<ul><li>Used to "push" an onscreen button.</li><li>Point to an onscreen element and push the left mouse button one time.</li><li>Hold the mouse still and click gently.</li></ul>
Drag	<ul><li>Used to move items around the screen, select text, and perform other tasks/commands.</li><li>Similar to a click, but do not let go of the mouse button.</li><li>Point to an onscreen element, click and hold down the left mouse button, and move the mouse until the onscreen element is in the desired location. This action is often referred to as *drag and drop*.</li></ul>
Double-click	<ul><li>Used to start a program or open a file/folder.</li><li>Point to an onscreen element and quickly click the left mouse button twice.</li><li>Hold the mouse still and click gently.</li><li>Be patient! A double-click doesn't have to be lightning fast, as you have about a second to complete the two clicks. Slowing down your clicking speed will help keep you from wiggling the mouse.</li></ul>
Right-click	<ul><li>Used to display a pop-up menu of options that relate to the object.</li><li>Point to an onscreen element and click the right mouse button once.</li><li>Dismiss a pop-up menu by (left) clicking another place on the screen or tapping Esc on the keyboard.</li></ul>

HANDS-ON 1.2 Use the Mouse

In this exercise, you will use the mouse to point at, click on, and drag around the Recycle Bin on the Desktop.

1. Follow these steps to start using the mouse:

Ⓐ Point with the mouse over the Recycle Bin.

Ⓑ Point away from the Recycle Bin.

Ⓒ Click (tap and release) with the left mouse button on the **Recycle Bin** icon.

Ⓓ Point away from the Recycle Bin (don't click) and notice that the icon stays selected (highlighted).

2. Follow these steps to drag the Recycle Bin to a new location on the Desktop:

Ⓐ Point at the Recycle Bin.

Ⓑ Press the left mouse button, and while keeping it depressed, move the mouse to drag the Recycle Bin to the right.

Ⓒ Release the mouse button at a new destination of your choice.

3. Drag the Recycle Bin back to its original location on the Desktop.

Note! Find the "Get Some Mousercise" link in the Chapter 1 section of the Student Resource Center to get more practice using the mouse.

Passwords and Account Settings

Every Windows user has their own login and password that allow them to connect to their various personal settings for the computer, as well as to other online accounts they may have that are connected to Windows.

Accessing Account Settings

The name of the person logged in to the computer is located at the top of the Start menu. This name and its circular "person" icon, which we will call the user icon/name button, opens the Settings window when clicked. Here you can access and change the various options related to your login account, such as your login information, password, your user account picture, and options for syncing your computer with other devices.

User icon/name button —

Account menu —

- **Sign-In Options:** From this screen you can change your password and set whether you need to enter your password again when you use your computer after it has been in **sleep mode**.

- **Work Access:** At work or school, you may be allowed to connect your personal computer to the network. If this is an option, you will be given specific instructions for how to do so.

- **Family & Other Users:** On a home computer, and if you have administrator privileges, you can add other users to the computer. The Add a Child button allows you to create accounts for children that have time limits on use and only allow visits to safe websites.

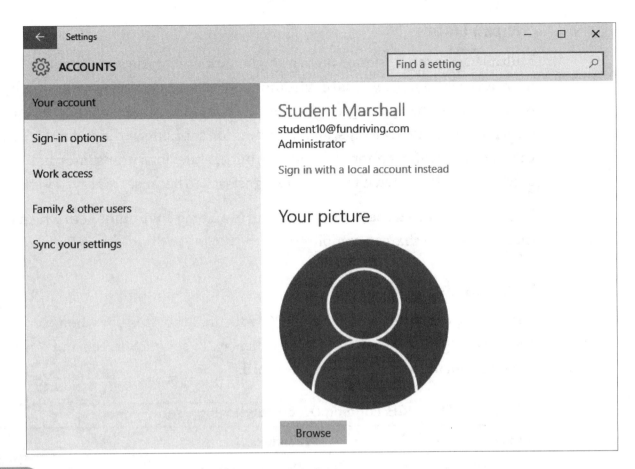

Warning! Never rely just on software to protect your kids online. Be proactive and teach them how to protect themselves.

- **Sync Your Settings:** This feature allows you to save various settings online that can be accessed from and transferred to other computers or devices like a tablet or smartphone using your login and password. This allows you to maintain the same look and feel across all your computers and devices.

Signing Out and Switching Users

Signing out of the computer is different from turning off the computer. Before signing out, you need to save your files to the hard drive. This is because when you do sign out, the computer closes the programs you were using and removes your login information and settings from memory so it will be ready for a new user to log on.

Note! Signing out does not shut off power to the computer; the computer is left running, and it is ready for another user to log in.

Switch Users

Multiple users can be signed on to a single computer at the same time, and each user can customize the visual environment of the computer to meet his or her needs. Unlike when you sign out, when you simply switch users, the previous user's information, screen settings, and programs are set aside in the computer's RAM, and the new user's information is employed, but the previous user's information can be quickly reimplemented if that person signs back in because it is saved in the RAM.

The ability to switch users is most helpful in a home environment in which more than one person shares a computer.

Locking the Computer

Locking the computer protects your PC from unauthorized use when you leave your desk. Locking causes the lock screen to display. To see your screen and continue working, you must re-enter your password.

QUICK REFERENCE: Logging Off and Switching Users

Task	Procedure
Log off Windows	▪ Click the Start button. ▪ Click your user icon/name button at the top of the menu and then click Sign Out.
Switch users	▪ Click the Start button. ▪ Click your user icon/name button at the top of the menu and then choose the desired user from the list.
Lock/Unlock Windows 10	▪ Click your user icon/name button and choose Lock. This will lock the computer and show the lock screen. ▪ To unlock the computer, click the lock screen and then enter your password on the sign-in screen when it appears.

HANDS-ON 1.3 Lock the Computer

In this exercise, you will give the lock command and then log back in using your own username and password.

1. Follow these steps to lock the computer:

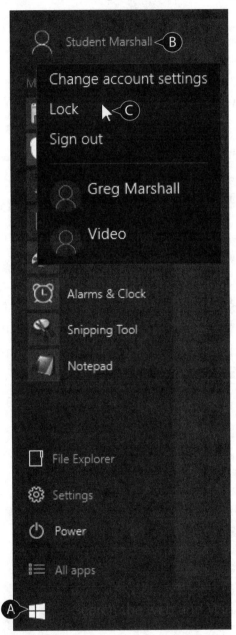

Ⓐ Click the **Start** button.

Ⓑ Click the **user icon/name** button.

Ⓒ Choose **Lock** from the menu.

There will be a pause as Windows prepares to display the lock screen. Wait for this screen to appear before continuing with the next step.

2. Click the **lock** screen.

3. Type your password in the password box and then tap ⌈Enter⌉ on the keyboard.
   After a pause, Windows returns you to the Desktop. You could just as easily have logged in as someone else by choosing their name from the corner of the login screen and entering their password.

The Start Menu

The Start menu is the one place you can go to launch most of the programs installed on your computer. Like all menus, the Start menu contains is a collection of **commands**, and these particular ones allow you to launch all of the programs that come with Windows 10. Commands on a menu often have a descriptive label and an icon. When you install a new program, Windows 10 adds a command for it to the Start menu.

Commands

A command is a link that can launch (start or open) a file, folder, or app, or that can execute a variety of other tasks. You might compare a command to a light switch on a wall used to turn on a ceiling light; clicking (or double-clicking) a command launches the object to which it is linked. More than one command can be linked to the same object. Commands can be located on the Desktop, in a menu, on a toolbar, or on a Ribbon.

HANDS-ON 1.4 Display and Dismiss the Start Menu

In this exercise, you will display and dismiss the Start menu using both the mouse and the keyboard.

1. Click the **Start** ⊞ button to display the Start menu.
   Note the left and right panes of the Start menu.

2. Click the **Start** ⊞ button again to dismiss the Start menu.

3. Press the **Windows** ⊞ key on the keyboard to display the Start menu.

4. Press the **Windows** ⊞ key again to dismiss the Start menu.
   It's easy to dismiss the Start menu if you pull it up by mistake.

Start Menu Panes

The Start menu is divided into left and right panes:

- The left pane contains a list of the most used commands and provides access to all apps on the computer as well as to account settings and options related to power settings.

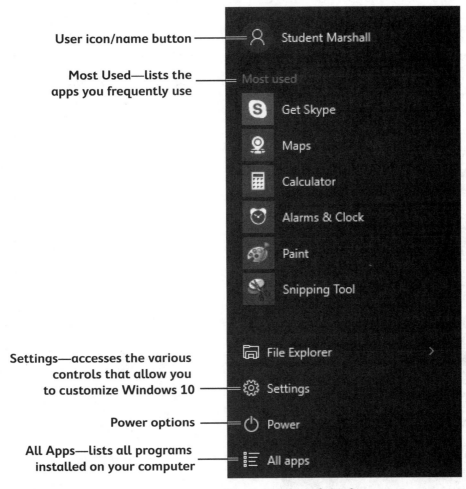

User icon/name button

Most Used—lists the apps you frequently use

Settings—accesses the various controls that allow you to customize Windows 10

Power options

All Apps—lists all programs installed on your computer

The left pane of the Start menu

- The right pane contains **live tiles** used to start programs as well as display personalized information. Live tiles can be organized and customized to suit your tastes and needs.

Tip! The appearance of the Start menu may vary depending on your version of Windows 10, but all Start menus function in the same manner.

You will notice that the terms app and program are used interchangeably. There is no longer a big difference between the two words, and both terms are used to describe a set of instructions that tell the computer or device to perform a specific task.

Tip! When you want to launch a frequently used program, first check for it in the Most Used programs section of the Start menu.

HANDS-ON 1.5 Launch a Program from the Start Menu

In this exercise, you will launch the Calculator app from the Start menu.

1. Use your mouse or the keyboard to display the Start menu.

2. Run your mouse pointer over the commands in the left pane and notice the selection bar that appears when your mouse pointer is above a command. *You can click anywhere within the selection bar to launch the command.*

3. Click the **All Apps** command.

4. Follow these steps to start the Calculator:

Ⓐ Drag the **scroll box** (at the top of the scroll bar) downward as necessary until you see the apps starting with "C."

Ⓑ Click **Calculator** to launch that app.

The Start menu will be dismissed, and after a short pause, the Calculator program will open on the Desktop.

5. Close the **Calculator** app by clicking the **Close** ⊠ button in the upper-right corner of the window.

Most Used Apps List

Windows 10 automatically adds commands for apps to the Most Used list in the Start menu. Sometimes an app is added to the list the first time you launch it. Other times you may need to use a program twice to have it added to the list. When the Most Used apps list becomes full, the command for the app that has been unused the longest is removed. You can also delete a command from the recently used program list.

Live Tiles

Live tiles are representations of apps that are used in place of icons in the Start menu. Unlike icons, various sizes of live tiles can be organized together on the screen based on user preference. When clicked, they launch the represented app.

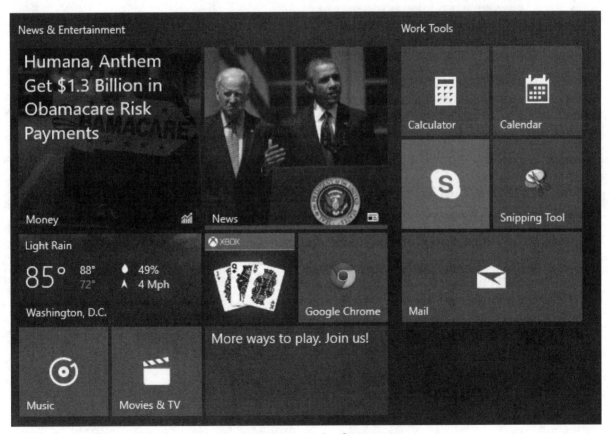

An example of live tiles sorted into two groups on the Start menu

Live tiles may also show information in them. A tile for a news app may show various news headlines, while the tile for a weather app may show weather information for your location. This information is updated via the Internet when a connection is available.

Not all apps will show information in their live tile.

Sizing Live Tiles

▶ View the video "Live Tiles" on the Student Resource Center at labyrinthelab.com/wtcb10.

Live tiles may be sized to one of four different sizes: Small, Medium, Wide, and Large. The size of the tile determines how much information is shown in the tile.

You may want to increase the size of the tiles that contain important information or that represent apps you frequently use, and make the tiles of less frequently used apps smaller.

As a live tile is sized smaller, less information is shown.

At the smallest setting, a live tile only shows the icon for the app it represents.

HANDS-ON 1.6 Resize a Live Tile

In this exercise, you will resize a live tile on the Start menu.

1. Click the **Start** ⊞ button to access the Start menu.

2. Right-click the **Photos** live tile and choose **Resize→Large**.

   If the Photos live tile is not available, choose another tile from the Start menu.

3. Right-click on the **Photos** live tile and change the size back to **Medium**.

. . . .

Turning Off Live Tiles

Live tiles can be turned off so that information is not shown in them. This may be helpful if you find the constantly changing tiles distracting or are not connected to the Internet to get updated information. To see current information, click on the tile to open the app or turn the tile back on.

The Weather app tile turned on and off.

HANDS-ON 1.7 Turn Off a Live Tile

In this exercise, you will turn off the live data to a tile.

1. Click the **Start** ⊞ button to access the Start menu.

2. Right-click the **News** tile and choose **Turn Live Tile Off**.

   If the News tile is not available, choose a different tile that has live data in it (such as the Money, Weather, or Sports tiles).

Notice that the tile appearance changes to the generic icon for the app.

3. Right-click the **News** tile and choose **Turn Live Tile On**.

   The live information is enabled again.

Pinning Commands to the Start Menu

Commands for any app can be easily **pinned** to the Start menu. Once a tile is pinned to the Start menu, it is easier to access and can be sized to suit your needs.

Tip! Tiles with live data (like News and Weather) work best in Wide and Large sizes, as the data being shown fits better on bigger tiles.

Moving Tiles on the Start Menu

Tiles can be moved around on the Start menu based on your preferences.

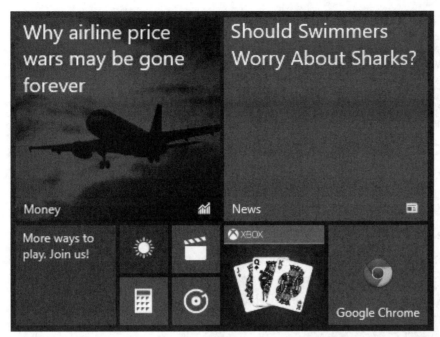

Different-sized tiles can be moved and organized together.

Tiles can also be moved into groups, and each group can be named. Grouping can make it easier to find individual apps.

These tiles are organized into two groups.

 HANDS-ON 1.8 Organize Live Tiles on the Start Menu

ON THE WEB

In this exercise, you will copy apps into the Start menu and organize them.

Before You Begin: This exercise runs on the Internet, so you need to know how to navigate it using a web browser. (The Internet is introduced in Chapter 6, Using the Internet.) Ask for assistance with step 1 if you don't yet know how to use the Internet.

1. Launch **Microsoft Edge** and type the following into the address bar: **labyrinthelab.com/wtcb10**. Tap Enter .

2. Click the **Chapter 1** heading to expand the menu and then click **Hands-On 1.8 Organize Live Tiles on the Start Menu**.

3. Click **All Apps** on the Start menu and find Calculator.

4. Right-click **Calculator** and choose **Pin to Start** on the menu that appears.
   The Calculator app will now appear as a live tile on the Start menu.

5. Find the **Calculator** live tile that you just created. Drag it to the top of the Start menu and release.
   Notice how the other tiles adjust their placement as you move the Calculator tile around.

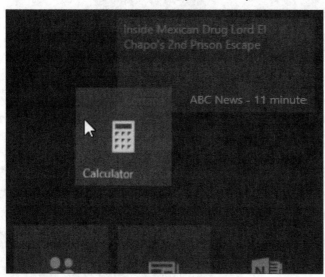

6. Right-click the **Calculator** tile and change the size to **Large**.
   Notice how the other tiles adjust to this change.

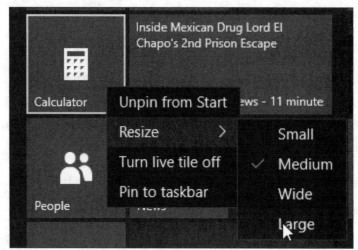

7. Right-click the **Calculator** tile and choose **Unpin from Start**.

8. Dismiss the Start menu using the mouse or the **Start** ⊞ button on the keyboard.

9. Click **Back to Course**.

Shutting Down

Windows is a very large collection of programs. If it is not shut down properly, you may discover upon restarting your computer that error messages appear—or even worse, that Windows won't start at all. This is because Windows needs time to properly shut down all of its software parts and pieces correctly, and just turning off the power doesn't allow enough time to do this.

Shut-Down Methods

There are three ways to shut down Windows, depending on what you want to do next. Available options are displayed via the Start button using the Power button and the Power menu:

- Shut Down

- Restart

- Sleep

Sleep

In sleep mode, the computer uses a lot less energy because the computer slows down. Any documents you are working on are saved, the processor works more slowly, the monitor is turned off, and other settings are triggered that allow the computer to save power.

Tip! On most laptops, closing the lid will immediately cause the laptop to go into sleep mode and start conserving battery power.

Shut Down

This command closes all programs, logs you out of the computer, and turns off its power. When you are done with the computer for the day, it is important to turn it off using the Shut Down command.

Warning! Never hold down the power button to turn a computer off unless you have no other choice. Windows needs time to close its various parts and pieces down properly, and turning the power off abruptly can corrupt parts of the Windows software and can even cause the computer to not be able to restart.

Restart

The restart mode closes all open program windows, logs you out, and powers down the computer. The computer then restarts and Windows reloads. Sometimes Windows will ask you to restart the computer after a new program or program update has been installed. That's because the new program can't be used until the system restarts and the new software is integrated into Windows.

QUICK REFERENCE: Shutting Down Windows

Task	Procedure
Shut down Windows and the computer	■ Close all open programs. ■ Click the Shut Down button (on the Power button menu).
Go into sleep mode	■ Choose Sleep from the Power button menu.
Exit sleep mode	■ Move the mouse or tap the Spacebar on your keyboard.

HANDS-ON 1.9 Use Sleep Mode and Shut Down

In this exercise, you will put the computer into sleep mode and then return it to working mode. Then you'll shut down Windows.

1. Make sure all programs are closed.

2. Follow these steps to go into sleep mode:

Ⓐ Click the **Start** button.

Ⓑ Click the **Power** button.

Ⓒ Choose **Sleep** from the menu.

Moving forward, steps like these will be written as "Click the Start button and then choose Power→Sleep."

3. Move the mouse or press the ⌷Spacebar⌷ to bring the computer out of sleep mode.

4. If the Start screen appears, click it. Enter your password when the login screen appears.
The computer is now ready to work again.

Shut Down Windows

5. Make sure any open programs are closed.

6. Click the **Start** ⊞ button and then choose **Power→Shut Down**.
It may take the computer 15 seconds or more to completely shut down.

Concepts Review

To check your knowledge of the key concepts introduced in this chapter, complete the Concepts Review quiz on this page. Or, you can take the quiz online by going to **labyrinthelab/wtcb10**.

Page number

1. Access to most features in Windows 10 is through the Start button located in the bottom-left corner of the screen.   **true false** _____

2. Icons are small pictures that represent programs or other features.   **true false** _____

3. Sleep mode is used to save energy when the computer is not going to be operated for a while.   **true false** _____

4. Drag and drop is used to move icons on the screen.   **true false** _____

5. It's okay to simply switch the power off when you're done using the computer.   **true false** _____

6. It is best for everyone to share one login and password on a computer.   **true false** _____

7. Which of these is the best password?

    a. Fido

    b. G476rty

    c. JohnSmith

    d. Password

    Page number: _____

8. Which of these IS NOT a mouse action?

    a. single-click

    b. double-click

    c. skip

    d. point

    Page number: _____

9. Which item IS NOT on the Power menu?

    a. Sleep

    b. Restart

    c. Shut Down

    d. Power System

    Page number: _____

10. Icons _____.

    a. are small images that can represent documents, photos, and apps

    b. can be found in many areas of Windows, including the Desktop and the taskbar

    c. act as the start buttons for programs

    d. All of the above

    Page number: _____

Skill Builders

....

SKILL BUILDER 1.1 Create Groups of Live Tiles

In this exercise, you will create groups of live tiles on the Start menu.

1. Launch **Edge** and navigate to the Student Resource Center: **labyrinthelab.com/wtcb10**

2. Click the **Chapter 1** heading to expand the menu and then click **Skill Builder 1.1 Create Groups of Live Tiles**.

3. Click the **Start** button.

4. Drag the edge of the **Start** menu to the right until it appears larger.

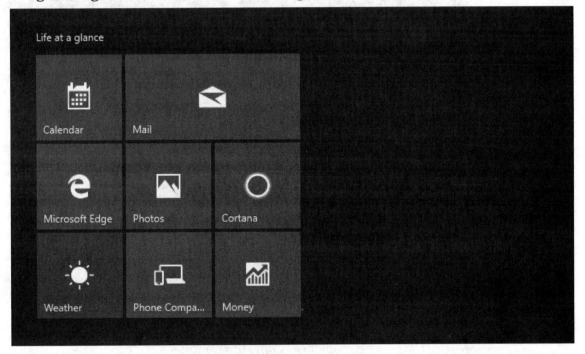

5. Drag the **Microsoft Edge** live tile into the blank area.
   Notice how the tile creates a new group. The blank heading is momentarily highlighted.

6. Drag the **Weather** tile so it is located next to the Edge tile.

7. Position your mouse above the Edge tile to bring up the text *Name group*, and then click on that text.

    You are now able to give the group of tiles a name.

8. Type **Information Apps** and press [Enter].

    Notice that your group of tiles now has a name.

9. Close the **Start** menu.

10. Click **Back to Course**.

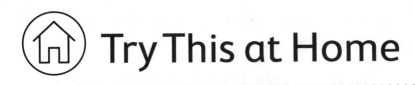 Try This at Home

TRY THIS AT HOME 1.1 Switch Users

In this exercise, you will switch from one user login to another.

Before You Begin: Skip this exercise if there is only one user listed on the Windows 10 login screen. You need at least two user accounts to switch between users.

1. Click the **Start** ⊞ button.

2. Follow these steps to switch users:

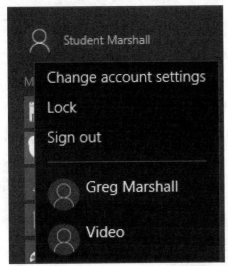

Ⓐ Click the **user icon/name** button.

Ⓑ Choose a different user from the list of users.
After a pause, Windows 10 displays the lock screen.

3. Type your password and then tap Enter .
Windows 10 will now make the switch. This can take 15 seconds or more to accomplish, depending on the speed of your computer and the amount of RAM available for the operation.

4. Switch back to your account by clicking the **user icon/name** button and choosing your login.
If you have not yet verified your account with Microsoft, at this point you may get a message that walks you through the process of verification.

5. Type your password and then tap Enter .
There will be another pause as Windows 10 switches you back to your Desktop. Notice that everything is just how you left it before switching to the other username.

TRY THIS AT HOME 1.2 Change Your Password

In this exercise, you will change your login password. This is the procedure used on your home computer, not on your school computers.

Note! This exercise may be performed live, but note that if you do this procedure outside of the WebSim, you will change the password to your online Microsoft Live account associated with this login. Please make sure to write down your new password if you complete this exercise live/outside the simulation.

1. Open **Microsoft Edge** and type the following into the address bar:
    `labyrinthelab.com/wtcb10`

2. Click the Chapter 1 heading to expand the menu, and then click **Try This at Home 1.2 Change Your Password**.

3. Click your login name on the top left-hand corner of the Start menu and then click **Change Account Settings** on the menu that appears.

4. In the Account Settings window, choose **Sign-In Options** from the menu on the left and then click the **Change** button under Password on the right.
    After a moment, a new window will appear, starting the password change procedure.

5. Enter your current password and click **Sign In**. In this simulation, your current password is **Student!12**.

6. Enter your current password in the space marked Old Password.

7. Your new password for this simulation is **College!3**. Enter the new password in the space marked Create Password. Enter it again in the space marked Reenter Password and click the **Next** button.

8. Click the **Finish** button to complete the procedure.

9. Click the **Close** ☒ button to shut the Account Settings window.

10. Click **Back to Course**.

TRY THIS AT HOME 1.3 Shut Down

In this exercise, you will shut down the computer properly.

1. Make sure that all of your open apps are closed.

2. From the Start menu choose **Power→Shut Down**.
   The computer will take a minute or two to complete its shutdown tasks. Be patient!

3. If the computer doesn't turn off the power automatically, you will need to manually power off the computer and the monitor.

Warning! Sometimes Windows will hang up when closing and will stop responding. It is best to give the computer a few minutes to correct the problem before turning the power off manually and overriding Windows.

CHAPTER 2

Starting and Controlling Apps

LEARNING OBJECTIVES

- Minimize, maximize, resize, and move app windows

- Use touch controls

- Describe the basic features of the Windows 10 taskbar

- Multitask effectively using the taskbar

- Access commands using the notification area

- Use the Action Center

Although apps (programs) from many different software companies are installed on your computer, the Windows operating system provides standardized tools for launching and controlling apps. In this chapter, you will become familiar with controlling an app window, using touch controls, working with the taskbar, and beginning to multitask by opening and switching between multiple programs.

📁 Case Study: Starting at the Beginning

William is going back to school and has bought a new computer to help him complete his homework. He has very little experience using a computer and feels a bit confused by all of the programs. He has tried clicking on the Desktop icons and has clicked on the Start menu, but the apps have so many different purposes: Several play music, one is like a checkbook, one is for drawing pictures, another is a notepad, and there also are card games. Before learning the different applications he will be using to do his homework, he decides to first learn what the programs have in common. If he can learn the standardized Windows 10 features used in most programs, it will be much easier to learn new apps. William starts by learning how to control the programs he has opened.

Controlling App Windows

Every app you open is displayed within its own window. This window, known as the app window, has controls and features that are similar in most programs. These basic controls are Windows standards; learn to use them in one app, and you will be able to work with similar controls in most new programs you use.

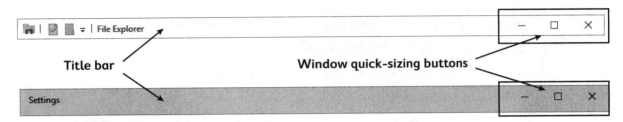

Here is an example of an app window for two different apps that come with Windows 10. The quick-sizing buttons and title bar are standard controls in all app windows.

Quick-Sizing Buttons

Quick-sizing buttons are used to reconfigure or close an app window. All apps use the same four quick-sizing buttons: Minimize, Maximize, Restore Down, and Close.

QUICK REFERENCE: Window Quick-Sizing Buttons

Button	Name	How It Works
—	Minimize	Removes the app window from the screen but continues to run it and leaves its app button on the taskbar
□	Maximize	Enlarges an app window to fill the screen
⧉	Restore Down	Resizes an app window to the smaller size it was before it was last maximized
×	Close	Exits an app
▮	App button (on taskbar)	Represents open apps (each has an image representing the app that is open)/minimizes an open window or reopens a window that has been minimized

The Minimize and Maximize Buttons

The Minimize $\boxed{-}$ button shrinks the app window from the Desktop, leaving only its app button on the taskbar. The app continues to run. To open the app window again to the size it was before it was minimized, click the app's button on the taskbar.

Tip! If an app window is open, you also can click its app button on the taskbar to minimize the window.

The Maximize □ button does just the opposite of the Minimize button. Maximize enlarges an app to fill the entire Desktop so that other programs become hidden behind it.

Why minimize or maximize programs? Having multiple programs open on your Desktop can be like having a messy desk. Minimizing windows will hide the distracting clutter of open windows, while maximizing a window will simply cover other opened windows.

Minimizing Versus Closing

The Minimize – button makes an app window shrink from the screen, but it does not close the app. If you are in the middle of a Spider Solitaire game and choose to minimize, the Spider Solitaire app button remains on the taskbar. When you click the app's taskbar button, the game will return to its previous size and be ready for you to play it.

When you click the Close × button, you end the card game and exit the app, and the app button is removed from the taskbar.

FROM THE KEYBOARD

Alt + F4 to close (exit) an app

Tip! A quick way to close a minimized app is to right-click the app button on the taskbar. This displays the control menu (shown in the figure), which includes a Close Window command at the bottom.

The Maximize and Restore Down Buttons

The center quick-sizing button toggles between the Maximize and Restore Down buttons depending on the state of the window; they are never shown at the same time. If you click Maximize, the center button changes to Restore Down. Conversely, if you click Restore Down, the center button changes to Maximize.

When you click the Maximize button...

... the center button changes to Restore Down.

When you click the Restore Down button...

... the center button changes to Maximize.

The App Button on the Taskbar

When an app is opened, its app button appears on the taskbar and displays the app's icon without a label. If you position the mouse cursor over the app button (without clicking), additional information about the app will be displayed in a ScreenTip. Clicking the app button allows you to minimize an open app window, restore a minimized window, or make an inactive app **active**.

HANDS-ON 2.1 Use Quick-Sizing Buttons

In this exercise, you will open the File Explorer and use the quick-sizing buttons to maximize, restore down, and minimize the app window.

1. Click the **Start** [icon] button and then choose **File Explorer**.

   The File Explorer app will open either maximized or in a restored-down size.

2. If the app window does not fill the screen, click the **Maximize** [icon] button.

   The app window enlarges to fill the entire Desktop (except for the taskbar). Also notice that the center quick-sizing button has changed to a Restore Down button.

Tip! It's usually a good idea to maximize any app window when it first opens to take full advantage of the entire screen.

3. Click the **Restore Down** [icon] button.

   Notice how the app window is restored back to its original, smaller size.

4. Click the **Minimize** [icon] button.

5. Click the **File Explorer** app button on the taskbar to restore the File Explorer program onto your Desktop.

Buttons on the taskbar help you identify the apps they are associated with. File Explorer, for example, uses a folder as its icon on the taskbar.

6. Click the **Close** ⨉ button to exit File Explorer.

· ·

Menu Button

Some apps have a menu button located on the top-left corner of the app, just below the title bar.

This button is generally used instead of a menu bar across the top of the app, and it contains commands and settings for the app.

Tip! Sometimes the menu button is referred to as the "hamburger button" because it looks a bit like a hamburger!

Moving and Resizing App Windows

App windows can be moved around on the Desktop the way you move papers and objects around your desk at home. Unlike your desk at home, though, app windows can be resized to fill the Desktop or reduced to a smaller size.

Title Bar

The title bar at the top of every app window serves several purposes. It displays the name of the app, and it also may display the name of the document or other object being edited by that app. Control buttons are located at the right and left ends of the bar.

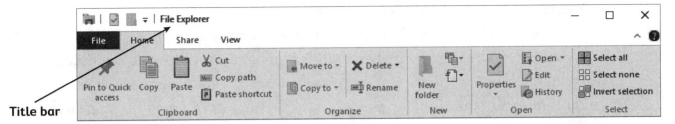

Title bar

Finally, the title bar provides a handle that can be used to move the app window. If you position the tip of your mouse pointer over any empty space on the title bar (not its border), you can hold down your left mouse button and drag an app window around the Desktop.

Resizing a Window

An app window has a narrow border surrounding it. You can resize a window by dragging the border from any side or any corner. Dragging a side border will resize only that side of the window. Dragging a corner will resize both sides attached to the corner.

If your mouse pointer will not change to a double-headed arrow when you point at a border, then the app window cannot be resized.

Some users find that resizing an app window is easier if they use the double-headed arrows that appear in the corner of the app window. These allow you to resize the app window in two directions at once.

The Snap Feature

Using the Snap feature is another way to maximize, restore down, or view two windows side by side on the Desktop. Snapping is accomplished by simply dragging windows to the top or sides of the Desktop.

Nonstandard App Windows

Although Windows establishes standards used by most programs, there are times when the standards are ignored or modified for appearance reasons or because certain functions are not necessary to use an app. In some programs the features are simply missing, while in other programs the features have a modified appearance or are grayed out and do not work.

QUICK REFERENCE: Resizing Windows Using Snap

Task	Procedure
Maximize a window	■ Click the title bar of a restored-down window and drag to the top edge of the Desktop until the mouse pointer touches it.
Restore down a window	■ Click the title bar and drag a maximized window away from the top edge of the Desktop.
Display two windows side by side	■ To make the window fill the left half of the Desktop, click the title bar and drag one window left until the mouse pointer touches the left edge of the Desktop.
	■ To make the window fill the right half of the Desktop, click the title bar and drag another window right until the mouse pointer touches the right edge of the Desktop.

HANDS-ON 2.2 Move, Resize, and Snap a Window

In this exercise, you will move, resize, and snap the File Explorer app window.

1. Choose **Start** ▦ and click **File Explorer** to launch.

2. If necessary, restore down the app window.

3. Click the title bar and drag the app window around the desktop.
   An app window cannot be resized using the mouse if it is maximized.

4. Practice resizing the app window using the borders or corners.

5. Initiate the Snap feature by using the title bar to drag the window to the left edge of the Desktop until the mouse pointer touches the edge.

6. Repeat step 5 by dragging the window to the right edge, the top edge, and finally away from all edges.

7. **Close** ⨯ the **File Explorer** app.

Touch Controls

▶ View the video "Touch Gestures" on the Student Resource Center at labyrinthelab.com/wtcb10.

Windows 10 supports the use of touch **gestures** on computers and devices that have touchscreens. Using touch, you can move and control objects on the screen using one, two, or three fingers. If you have a precision touchpad on your laptop, you will be able to use these advanced controls.

HANDS-ON 2.3 How Can I Tell If I Have a Touchscreen?

In this exercise, you will check to see if your Windows 10 computer has a touchscreen.

1. Choose **Start** ⊞ and select **Settings**.

2. From Settings, double-click the **System** icon.

System
Display, notifications,
apps, power

3. On the Systems page, click **About** on the left side of the screen. On the right side of the screen, look for the text *Pen and touch*. The text to the right will tell you whether your computer supports touch gestures.

Edition	Windows 10 Pro Insider Preview
Product ID	00362-10000-00000-AA525
Processor	AMD E1-2100 APU with Radeon(TM) HD Graphics 1.00 GHz
Installed RAM	8.00 GB (7.45 GB usable)
System type	64-bit operating system, x64-based processor
Pen and touch	No pen or touch input is available for this display

This computer does not support touch gestures.

4. Close ⌷×⌷ the window.

Touch Gestures

Touch gestures that involve moving a finger across the screen of your laptop or device while your finger is lightly touching the screen give the computer commands. The following are some examples.

QUICK REFERENCE: Using Touch Gestures

Task	Procedure	
Open the Action Center	▪ Swipe in from the right edge of the screen.	
Open Task view	▪ Swipe in from the left edge of the screen.	
View the title bar	▪ Swipe down from the top of the screen. This allows you to view an app's title bar when in full-screen view. Not all apps have a hidden title bar to view.	
View the taskbar	▪ Swipe up from the bottom of the screen.	
Open, select, or activate an item	▪ Tap once on the item.	
Zoom in or out	▪ Touch the screen with two or more fingers and drag them toward or away from each other.	

Illustrations provided by GestureWorks® (www.gestureworks.com)

Touchpad Controls

The touchpad on your laptop or device can do more than just point and click! The following special finger movements enhance your ability to control items on the screen.

QUICK REFERENCE: Using Touch Gestures

Task	Procedure	
Open the Task screen	■ Swipe three fingers upward on the touchpad.	
Show the Desktop	■ Swipe three fingers downward on the touchpad.	
Switch between open windows	■ Swipe three fingers right or left on the screen. This slowly flips between all open programs.	

Working with the Taskbar

The taskbar runs the width of the Desktop at the bottom of the screen. The center section of the taskbar displays the programs that are open.

Only one app window can be active at a time, and it will be displayed in front of the other inactive programs open on your Desktop. The active app button will have a highlighted box around it. Clicking on an inactive app button will make that app active and the computer will move its window in front of others on the Desktop.

Active app button
(will have light color box around it)

Pinned programs

The notification area

Inactive app button

Show Desktop button

Notification Area

The notification area on the right end of the taskbar has four primary functions.

- It displays the system clock and current date.

- It displays icons representing tasks and functions that are running in the background, such as antivirus software.

- It displays notifications of system events, such as app updates.

- It provides access to some of the apps that have icons displayed.

HANDS-ON 2.4 Change Taskbar Settings

In this exercise, you will open the taskbar and Start menu Properties dialog box to observe setting options and to make changes to the taskbar settings.

1. Follow these steps to display the Taskbar and Start menu Properties window:

    A Right-click a clear portion of the taskbar to display its pop-up menu.

    B Choose **Properties**.

2. When the Taskbar and Start menu Properties dialog box appears, follow these steps to change the taskbar's appearance:

    A Click the **Taskbar** tab.

    B Click once (do not double-click) the Use Small Taskbar Buttons option box to place a checkmark in the box.

    C Click **Apply** (not OK) near the bottom of the dialog box.

    This makes the icons smaller, which enables more app buttons to be displayed on the taskbar. However, notice that the current date is no longer displayed in the notification area.

Tip! The Apply button makes the changes but leaves the dialog box open. The OK button applies the changes but also closes the box.

3. Remove the checkmark next to the Use Small Taskbar Buttons option box and click **Apply** again.
Notice that larger icons have been restored on the taskbar.

4. Click **OK** to close the dialog box.

Pinning and Unpinning Apps

Windows 10 allows you to pin app buttons to the taskbar in much the same way you pin programs to the Start menu. Pinning enables you to put your most-used apps on the taskbar where they are easier to find and launch. Typically, the taskbar is set to be displayed even when windows are maximized, which means that the pinned app buttons are always available. A pinned app that is not currently open will not have a square button border around its icon.

Pinned app buttons do not have borders when the app is closed.

QUICK REFERENCE: Pinning and Unpinning Programs

Task	Procedure
Pin an app	■ On the Start menu, right-click on the app button to display a pop-up menu.
	■ Choose Pin to Taskbar.
	■ The app button will remain on the taskbar even when the app is closed until it is unpinned.
Unpin an app	■ Right-click on the app button to display a pop-up menu.
	■ Choose Unpin This App from Taskbar.

Tip! Having too many pinned apps on the taskbar can make it difficult to tell what programs are open and can cause confusion when you try to work with multiple apps.

HANDS-ON 2.5 Pin and Unpin an App

In this exercise, you will open Notepad, pin the app to the taskbar, and then unpin the app from the taskbar.

1. Choose **Start → All Apps**.

2. Scroll down thru the apps and click **Windows Accessories → Notepad**.

3. Follow these step to pin the app to the taskbar:

A Right-click the app button on the taskbar.

B Choose **Pin This Program to Taskbar** from the menu.

C Right-click the app button again.

D Choose **Close Window** from the menu.

The Notepad icon remains on the taskbar. Once the app is closed, it no longer has a button border around it.

4. Follow these steps to unpin the Notepad app:

A Right-click the app button.

B Choose **Unpin This Program from Taskbar**.

The Notepad icon is removed from the taskbar.

Action Center (Notifications)

The Action Center provides a central location for information being shared by various apps in your computer. These notifications can be varied, from news alerts from your News app, to updates from Windows 10.

The Action Center is accessed by clicking the Notification button in the notification area.

Click the Notification button to bring up the Action Center.

FROM THE KEYBOARD

⊞+A to open the Action Center

Notifications

Notifications vary depending on the app. When highlighted with your mouse, individual notifications can be deleted by using the Close button.

A specific section can be closed the same way. Notifications related to individual programs and various areas of Windows 10 can be turned on and off in Settings.

HANDS-ON 2.6 Set Notifications

In this exercise, you will turn notifications off and then back on.

1. Choose **Start → Settings** and then click the **System** icon.

2. From the left side of the System window, choose **Notifications & Actions**.
   Notice the options that appear on the right side of the screen.

3. Click the **On/Off** slider under Show App Notifications to turn them off.

Show app notifications

 Off

   The Notification button in the notification area on the taskbar now has a small minus sign in the bottom corner. When you hover your mouse pointer over the icon, the ScreenTip indicates that new notifications will not appear.

   New notifications (Off)

   1:05 PM
   7/8/2015

4. Click the **On/Off** slider under Show App Notifications to turn notifications back on.
   Scroll down through the Notifications & Actions window and notice you can turn notifications off for individual apps. Note that the Notification button in the notification area on the taskbar no longer has a small minus sign.

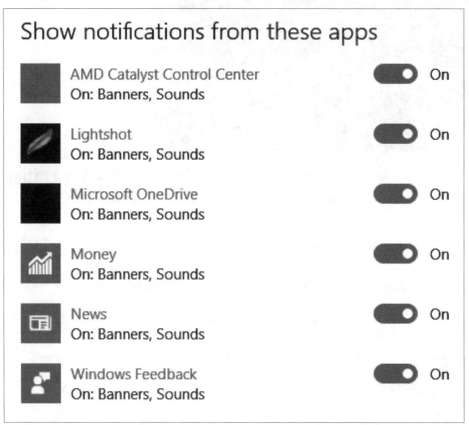

Show notifications from these apps

AMD Catalyst Control Center   On
On: Banners, Sounds

Lightshot   On
On: Banners, Sounds

Microsoft OneDrive   On
On: Banners, Sounds

Money   On
On: Banners, Sounds

News   On
On: Banners, Sounds

Windows Feedback   On
On: Banners, Sounds

5. Close the **Settings** window.

Actions

The Action Center contains rows of icons, or actions, along the bottom that enable you to quickly access various settings on your computer.

When the actions are collapsed, you are left with four quick actions. These four actions can be configured in the Settings to access the specific features of your choosing.

Multitasking

One useful feature of Windows is its ability to multitask. Multitasking enables the computer to run multiple programs or operations at the same time. Multitasking lets Windows run various tasks and activities in the background that you might not even be aware of, such as downloading software patches, monitoring the security of your computer, and performing hundreds of other small tasks. You also can take advantage of multitasking to help you to become more efficient with your time in front of the computer; you can have several programs open, print a document, and listen to music—all at the same time.

Multitasking lets you perform many tasks simultaneously: check email, pay bills online, listen to music, and print documents.

HANDS-ON 2.7 Open Multiple Programs

In this exercise, you will open three programs from the Start menu and watch the app buttons be added to the taskbar.

1. Click **Start**.

   Review the commands in the recently used programs list in the left pane.

2. Click **Calculator** if available in the left pane or choose **All Apps → Windows Accessories**.

   Notice the app button has been added to the taskbar.

3. Open **Notepad** from the Windows Accessories listing.

4. Open **Paint** from the Windows Accessories listing.

   There are now three app buttons on the taskbar.

   Leave these programs open for the next exercise.

App Switching

You can easily switch between open programs (when multitasking) using one of several switching tools. Windows often offers more than one way to complete a task. To make an app active, you can use the app window, the app buttons, the keyboard, or the Task View button.

Which App Is Active?

There is a rule when running multiple programs: You can work in only one app at a time. If you think of open app windows like objects on your desk, the object you are currently using would be the active object and would, most likely, be on top of the other objects.

Windows places the active app window in front (on top) of the inactive windows. The app button on the taskbar is brighter.

The active app button is brighter.

Inactive buttons are darker in color.

HANDS-ON 2.8 Switch Programs

In this exercise, you will change the active app window by clicking on inactive app windows and app buttons located on the taskbar.

Before You Begin: Three programs (Calculator, Notepad, and Paint) should still be open on the Desktop.

1. Follow these steps to make Calculator the active app:

Ⓐ If necessary, restore down [❑], resize, and move the windows to approximate the way they look here.

Ⓑ If Calculator is not active, click the **Calculator** app button to make it the active app.

2. Follow these steps to change the active app:

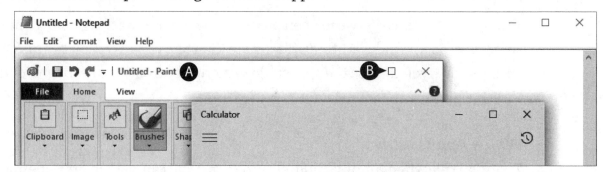

A Click a visible part of the Paint window to make the window and the app button active.

B Click the **Maximize** button to make the Paint window cover the Desktop.

C Although Paint is hiding the other programs, click the **Calculator** app button to make it active.

If any part of an inactive window can be seen, clicking the window will make it active, but avoid clicking its Close button! If windows are maximized, use the app buttons to make other programs active.

3. Make **Notepad** active and click the **Close** button to exit the app.

Leave Calculator and Paint open.

The Flip Command

The **Flip** command enables you to quickly switch or "flip" between open programs. You access the command using the keyboard.

FROM THE KEYBOARD

Alt + Tab to switch between opened programs

In the Task-Switching box, large icons are displayed for open programs.

 Tip! The Flip command is the quickest way to switch between open programs while keeping your hands on the keyboard.

QUICK REFERENCE: Switching Programs Using Flip

Task	Procedure
Use the Flip command	■ Hold down Alt and tap Tab to display the Flip window.
	■ While continuing to hold down Alt, keep tapping Tab until the icon for the app you want to use is selected.
	■ Release Alt. The app window you chose is now active.

🖱 HANDS-ON 2.9 Flip Between Active Programs

In this exercise, you will flip (switch) between Calculator, Paint, and the Notepad.

1. Start **Notepad**.

2. Make **Paint** the active app if it is inactive.

3. Hold down the ⌷Alt⌷ key on the keyboard and keep it held down until step 5. (Use your left thumb so you can tap the ⌷Tab⌷ key in the next step.)

4. Tap the ⌷Tab⌷ key once (while continuing to hold down ⌷Alt⌷).
   The Task-Switching box appears. The order of the icons for open programs can be different and will change depending on which app was active when you gave the Flip command.

5. While holding down the ⌷Alt⌷ key, tap the ⌷Tab⌷ key until **Calculator** is chosen in the Task Switcher window, as shown here.

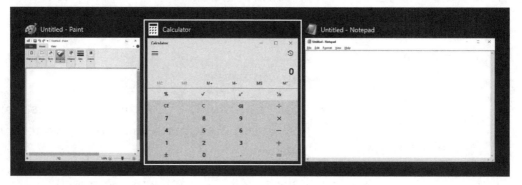

6. Release the ⌷Alt⌷ key.
   The Calculator app becomes active and jumps to the front of the Desktop.

7. Practice using ⌷Alt⌷+⌷Tab⌷ to switch between programs.
   Leave Calculator, Notepad, and Paint open.

Show Desktop and Task View

Windows 10 provides other features to help you navigate between multiple windows in quick and efficient ways:

Show Desktop button—The Show Desktop button is located at the far right end of the taskbar. It helps you quickly clear the Desktop of window clutter, because instead of minimizing one window at a time, you can minimize all windows at the same time.

 Task View button—The Task View button enables you to choose among your open apps without having to hold down multiple buttons on the keyboard like Flip requires.

When the Task View button is clicked on the taskbar, a screen showing all open apps appears, including a live view of what's running in each app. Clicking on a specific app makes it live on the screen.

HANDS-ON 2.10 Use Task View

In this exercise, you will use the Task View button to switch between running apps.

Before You Begin: Three apps (Calculator, Notepad, and Paint) should still be open on the Desktop.

1. Click on the **Paint** app to make it the active app.

2. Click the **Task View** button on the taskbar.

3. Click **Calculator** in the Task View window.
   Notice that the Calculator app is now the active app on the Desktop.

4. Practice using the Task View button to switch between open apps.

5. Close the **Calculator**, **Notepad**, and **Paint** apps.

The Usefulness of Multitasking

Multitasking—the ability to perform more than one task at a time—is a powerful tool. Coupled with today's sophisticated processors, large monitors, and Windows 10's new features, multitasking can make your work time more efficient and your personal time more fun.

Before the advent of Microsoft Windows, PCs could run only one app at a time. If you were printing a long document from an older PC, you had to wait for the job to finish before you could check your email or continue playing Solitaire.

Windows 10 has increased multitasking capabilities over its predecessors that enable a multitude of processes to run in the background, such as antivirus protection, automatic updates, and messaging. At the same time, you can be printing a document, downloading a movie from the Internet, catching up on your email, and listening to music.

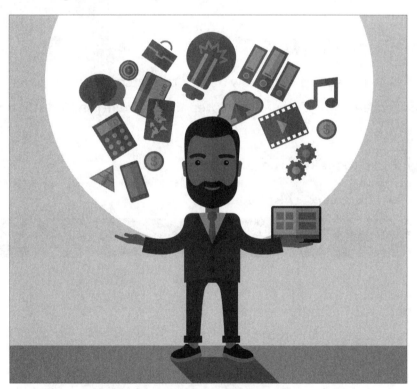

Multitasking allows you to perform many tasks simultaneously, such as checking email, paying bills online, listening to music, and printing documents.

Concepts Review

To check your knowledge of the key concepts introduced in this chapter, complete the Concepts Review quiz on this page. Or, you can take the quiz online by going to **labyrinthelab/wtcb10**.

Page number

1. Touch gestures are special finger movements used with the touchscreen on a laptop.

    true false _____

2. Multitasking enables you to run more than one app at a time.

    true false _____

3. The Show Desktop button maximizes all open apps.

    true false _____

4. If you open three programs, you will have three active app windows.

    true false _____

5. Task View allows you to choose between apps without holding down multiple keyboard buttons.

    true false _____

6. Using the Minimize, Maximize, and Restore Down buttons to resize a window is called multitasking.

    true false _____

7. Which IS NOT a quick-sizing button?

    a. ×

    b. −

    c. ▫

    d. ⧉

    e. None of the above

    Page number: _____

8. Which button minimizes a window?

    a. ×

    b. −

    c. ▫

    d. ⧉

    e. None of the above

    Page number: _____

9. How can you tell if an app is active?

    a. Its window is the biggest.

    b. Its name is grayed out in the title bar.

    c. Its app button looks brighter on the taskbar.

    d. All of the above

    Page number: _____

10. Which IS NOT a touch gesture?

    a. open Task view

    b. zoom in

    c. open help app

    d. zoom out

    Page number: _____

Skill Builders

SKILL BUILDER 2.1 **Resize and Move Apps**

In this exercise, you will resize and move the Calculator on the Desktop.

1. Start the **Calculator** app.

2. Maximize the app using the **Maximize** ▫ button.

3. Restore down the Calculator app.

4. Click in the title bar of Calculator and drag it to a new position on the screen.

5. Minimize the Calculator window.

6. Click the **Calculator** button on the taskbar to restore it to the Desktop.

7. Close the **Calculator** app.

SKILL BUILDER 2.2 **Pin and Unpin Apps**

In this exercise, you will pin two commands to the Start menu and use commands to launch both apps. Finally, you will unpin the commands from the Start menu.

1. Choose **Start** ⊞→**All Apps**→**Windows Accessories**.

2. Right-click the **Notepad** and **Paint** items to pin these commands to the live tile area of the Start menu.

3. Click the **Back** command to close all apps.
   The Back command closes all apps, so you can view the Most Used and the live tiles. Notice that the newly pinned programs appear on the Start menu as tiles.

Launch Pinned Programs

4. Launch **Notepad** using the new tile. Depending on how many tiles are on your Start screen, you may need to scroll down the Start screen or resize the window.

5. Launch **Paint** using the new Paint tile.

Leave the programs open on the Desktop for the next exercise.

Remove the New Commands

6. Open the **Start** ⊞ menu.

7. Right-click the **Notepad** tile and the **Paint** tile and unpin their tiles from the Start menu's live tiles.

8. Dismiss the **Start** menu.

. . . .

SKILL BUILDER 2.3 Multitask

In this exercise, you multitask by using the control features discussed in this chapter.
Before You Begin: Notepad and Paint should still be open.

1. Click the **Notepad** app button on the taskbar to make it active.

Notepad jumps in front of the other window, and its title bar changes to show it is the active app. Also notice that Notepad's taskbar button appears brighter than the other app's button.

2. Click the **Paint** app button on the taskbar to make it active.

3. **Maximize** ◻ the Paint window.

Let's say you want to make Notepad the active app again. Because Notepad is hidden under Paint, you need to use its taskbar button to make the app active.

4. Click the **Notepad** app button on the taskbar to make Notepad active.

The Notepad window pops up on top of the Paint window, ready for you to type in it.

5. **Maximize** ◻ the Notepad window.

6. **Restore Down** ◱ each app.

Each app now has a window size that partially fills the Desktop.

7. Practice resizing and moving each app window.

8. Minimize both programs at the same time using the **Show Desktop** button at the right end of the taskbar.

The purpose of the Show Desktop button is to minimize all open programs with a single click, giving you quick access to the Desktop.

9. Follow these steps to quickly close the minimized Notepad app:

Ⓐ Right-click the app button to display the control menu.

Ⓑ Choose **Close Window**.

10. Use the same right-click method on the Paint taskbar button to close its window.

CHAPTER 3

Creating an Online Account

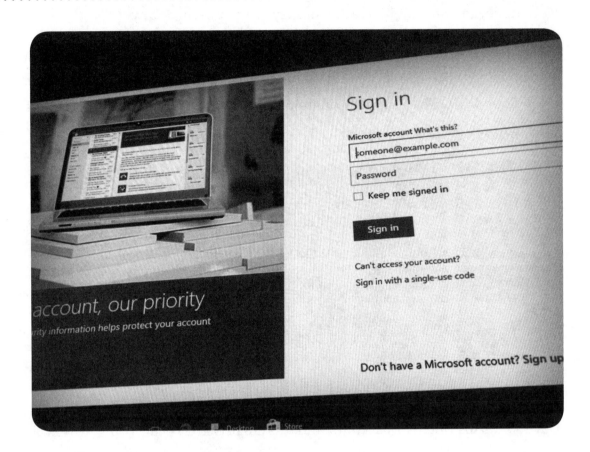

LEARNING OBJECTIVES

- Describe why we use online resources
- Understand the basics of cloud computing
- Create a free Microsoft account
- Connect your Microsoft account to Windows 10
- Understand account verification

Online apps give you the ability to work anywhere on any computer or device, such as a phone or tablet. With online storage, you can also access your files anywhere from any device that is linked to the Internet. In this chapter, you will learn about online apps and storage. You'll also set up your own free Microsoft account.

Learning Resources: **labyrinthelab.com/wtcb10**

📁 Case Study: Going Online

Dave was upset. His new computer didn't have any apps to help him get his school work done, and he didn't have any money left to purchase any.

Dave's friend Greg suggested that Dave get a free Microsoft account. "With a Microsoft account, you can access many great apps straight from the Internet at no cost," Greg said. "The apps are not as powerful as the ones you would purchase, but they help you get your school work done."

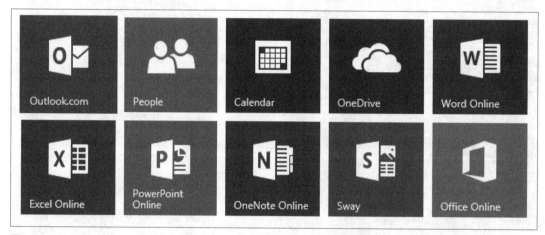

The various apps available when you sign up for a Microsoft account

Dave set up his Microsoft account and was surprised by everything he was able to do. Soon, Dave was creating documents and presentations, and receiving email. He was also able to store all his files online.

It didn't take long for Dave to become a productive online app–using student!

Note! This is a special chapter designed to get you signed up for a Microsoft account that can be used throughout the remainder of this book. This chapter is shorter than the others and does not contain the Hands-On and Skill Builder exercises used in the other chapters.

Why Online?

The Internet has grown from a tool for sending messages and doing research into a vast system with unlimited possibilities. As the access to and size of online storage has expanded exponentially, access speeds have increased and the number of access points has multiplied. As a result, you now are able to store all your apps, documents, music, pictures, and more online and also access your work from any computer or device that's connected to the Internet.

The Cloud

The cloud, or **cloud computing**, generally refers to the storage of apps and services on the Internet so they can be accessed from anywhere by your computers and devices that have Internet access. Many of the apps in Windows 10 are cloud based and require a connection to the Internet to function.

There are many online **cloud storage** providers including Microsoft OneDrive, Dropbox, Google Drive, box, and more.

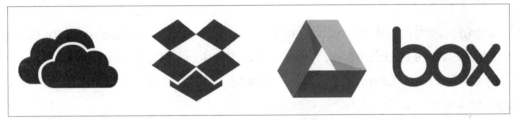

The logos for four popular cloud storage sites: Microsoft OneDrive, Dropbox, Google Drive, and box.

Microsoft Office Online

Microsoft offers a number of apps that are completely online—and free. They include online storage with OneDrive and a suite of programs called Office Online. With these, you can work on your documents and files, store your files online, and access them from any computer or device, including your smartphone! These online apps are free to use, and some of them are used in this book.

Office Online apps offer basic functionality, and more complete versions can be purchased if needed.

Creating Your Microsoft Account

▶ View the video "Creating Your Microsoft Account" on the Student Resource Center at labyrinthelab.com/wtcb10.

Creating an online Microsoft account is simple and will enable you to complete many of the exercises in this book. If you have Windows 10 already installed on a home computer or have used one of the many Microsoft online services, you may already have an account.

If you already have a Microsoft account, use that account in this chapter and throughout this book.

Account Verification

Once your account information has been accepted, Microsoft will send a verification to your email address. This is a security check to make sure you are the one who created the account.

Clicking the verify link in the email completes the verification process and unlocks all the features of your Microsoft account.

ACCOUNTS AND APPS

Account/App	What Is It For?
Windows 10 login	Sign on to the computer
Microsoft account	Allows access to OneDrive and Office Online; needs to be connected with your Windows login
OneDrive	Microsoft's free online storage option and the starting point for accessing Office Online apps in this book
Office Online	Free basic versions of some of Microsoft's apps

HANDS-ON 3.1 Create a Microsoft Online Account

In this exercise, you will create a Microsoft Online account that will be used throughout this book.

Before You Begin: Make sure you have an email address that you can use and check. If you don't have an email address, ask your instructor for help.

1. Start the **Microsoft Edge** browser by clicking the icon on the taskbar.

2. **Maximize** ☐ the browser window.

3. Click in the blank area below the Close button (on the Start tab) and next to the Refresh button to make the address bar appear.

4. In the address bar, type **account.microsoft.com** and tap Enter .

5. Click the **Create Account** button near the bottom of the window.

One account for all things Microsoft

Sign in to manage your info, your purchases, your family's devices, your security and privacy. It's all tied together with your Microsoft account.

Sign in   Create account

6. Fill out the account creation form.

   Your username is any email address you would like to use. Remember to note the account password that you create so you will be able to access your Microsoft account at a later date.

Tip!   Use the ⌈Tab⌉ key to move between form fields.

7. Enter the numbers and letters that you see in the captcha image at the bottom of the page and click the **Create Account** button.

   Captchas are used to make sure you are a real person and not a computer attempting to make hundreds of accounts.

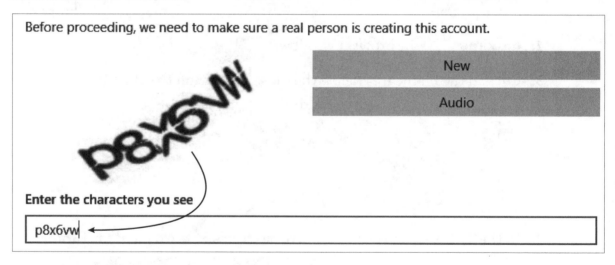

Before proceeding, we need to make sure a real person is creating this account.

New

Audio

Enter the characters you see

p8x6vw

8. Close **Edge**.

Verify Your Account

9. Access your email and look for a new email from the Microsoft account team.

10. Click the **Verify** button in the email to verify your account setup.

   Your Internet browser will start, and a web page with a message will appear telling you the verification was a success.

Microsoft account

Verify your email address

To finish setting up this Microsoft account, we just need to make sure this email address is yours.

Or you may be asked to enter this security code: **1200**

If you didn't make this request, click here to cancel.

Thanks,
The Microsoft account team

11. Click **OK**.

You will be taken to your Microsoft account page.

Ready to go!

Thanks for verifying student4@fundriving.com. You can now get back to what you were doing.

OK

12. Close **Edge**.

. . . .

Making Connections

Your Microsoft account must be connected to the Windows 10 login you use to sign on to the computer. This connection allows Windows 10 to automatically connect you to various apps without constantly asking for your login information. Many of the apps that come with Windows 10 will automatically connect to your Microsoft account as well.

HANDS-ON 3.2 Connect Accounts

In this exercise, you will connect your newly created Microsoft account to your Windows 10 login.

Before You Begin: Make sure you are logged in with your login and not that of another student.

1. In the Start menu, click on your **user icon/name** button and then on **Change Account Settings**.

2. Click **Your Account** on the left-side of the Accounts screen. Scroll down the window to the bottom.

3. Under **Other Accounts You Use**, click **Add a Microsoft Account**.

4. Enter your email and password that you created in the previous exercise and click the **Sign In** button.

   After a moment, your Microsoft account will be connected to your computer and will be shown on your account screen.

5. Close the **Accounts** window.

Logging In to OneDrive and Online Apps

Now that you have a Microsoft account, you can use it to log in to OneDrive and Microsoft Office online. OneDrive is your online file storage and the starting point for logging in to the other online Microsoft apps that are used in this book.

Online Messages

When using a browser and online apps, you may get messages on the screen that are not part of the content of this book but rather a normal part of the online experience.

Would you like to save your password for live.com?
More info

Yes   No   ×

Sometimes the browser will ask if you want to save the password you have just entered. In most cases, you will want to click no and continue on with your work.

When logging in to Microsoft Online apps, you may get a "What's New" message that will tell you about new features that have been added. These messages can be closed by clicking the "Got It!" button.

Tip!   It's common for messages to show up on the screen. After reading them, click Close × or OK.

HANDS-ON 3.3 Log In to OneDrive

In this exercise, you will log in to OneDrive. This is the process you will follow each time.

Before you begin: Make sure you have created a Microsoft account in Hands-On 3.1 and have the login and password from that exercise.

1. Start the **Edge** browser by clicking the icon on the taskbar.

2. **Maximize** □ the browser window.

3. Click in the blank area below the Close button (on the Start tab) and next to the Refresh button to make the address bar appear.

4. Type **onedrive.live.com** in the address bar and tap Enter .

Are You Already Logged In?

If you have connected your Microsoft account to your Windows 10 login, you may find that you are already logged in to OneDrive. Use these steps to verify that your Microsoft account is the one that is logged in.

5. Click the **user icon** button on the right-hand end of OneDrive and verify whether you are logged in.

- If it's your login, awesome! Go to step 10.

- If it's not your login, click **Sign Out** and go to step 6.

- If no one is logged in and OneDrive is not open, go to step 7.

6. Enter your email address and password in the space provided, and click the **Sign In** button.

Basic Login

If you are signing in as a guest on Windows 10 or have not yet connected your Windows account to your Windows 10 login, you will start the sign-in process at the "splash" screen for OneDrive.

7. Click the **Sign In** button in the right corner of the **OneDrive** screen.

8. Enter the email address you used for your Microsoft account and click **Next**.

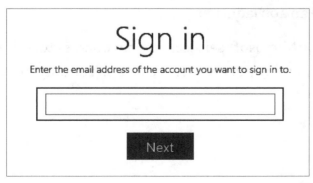

9. Enter your password and click **Sign In**.

10. When done with OneDrive, click the **Close** ⨯ button to exit **Edge**.

. . . .

Always Logged In

Once you have created your Microsoft account and opened OneDrive, Windows 10 should remember your login and automatically start OneDrive when accessed. You should only have to use your login and password in these situations:

- when accessing it from a browser in the library

- when your Microsoft account is not connected to your login

- when using any computer or device that is not your own

Opening Microsoft Office Online Apps

Once you have logged in to OneDrive, you can open any of the Microsoft online apps by clicking the app's button located on the left-side of the online app's title bar. All Microsoft online apps feature an app launcher.

The app launcher lists all of the Microsoft services you have access to. Clicking a service on the button starts a new browser tab with that app running in it.

HANDS-ON 3.4 Start Word Online

In this exercise, you will go to OneDrive online and start Microsoft Word Online.

1. Start the **Edge** browser by clicking its icon on the taskbar.

2. **Maximize** ⬜ the browser window.

3. Click in the blank area below the Close button (on the Start tab) and next to Refresh to make the address bar appear.

4. Type **onedrive.live.com** in the address bar and tap ⬚Enter⬚.

5. Log in to **OneDrive** if not already logged in.

   Refer to Hands-On 3.3 if you need a reminder about doing this.

6. Click the **app launcher** button on the left side of the OneDrive title bar and choose **Word Online** from the menu that appears.

Notice that the browser changes to Word Online.

Note! Remember, if the "What's New" window appears, simply click *Got It!* to close.

7. Choose the **New Blank Document** option.

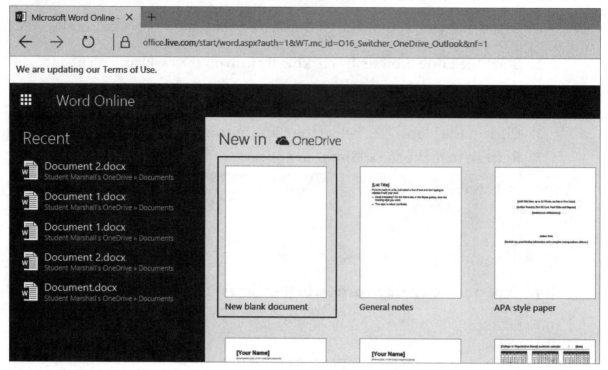

You are now in Word Online and are ready to write.

8. Exit **Edge** using the **Close** ☒ button. This also closes Word Online, which is open within the browser window.

Concepts Review

To check your knowledge of the key concepts introduced in this chapter, complete the Concepts Review quiz on this page. Or, you can take the quiz online by going to **labyrinthelab/wtcb10**.

Page number

1. The cloud refers to the WiFi network in your home.   **true false** _____

2. Account verification makes sure you are the one who created the Microsoft account.   **true false** _____

3. Captchas are used to make sure you are a real person.   **true false** _____

4. By connecting your Microsoft account to Windows 10, many additional apps will be able to connect to your account automatically.   **true false** _____

5. Storing your files in the cloud allows you to access them from anywhere.   **true false** _____

6. Which app IS NOT a free app that your Microsoft Account gives you access to?

    a. Excel Online

    b. Publisher Online

    c. Word Online

    d. Outlook.com

    Page number: _____

7. When do you need to log into OneDrive?

    a. when a guest on a friend's computer

    b. when accessing from a browser in the library

    c. when your Microsoft account is not connected to your login

    d. All of the above

    Page number: _____

CHAPTER 4

Working with Apps

LEARNING OBJECTIVES

- Use common features found in drop-down menus, on toolbars and Ribbons, and on scroll bars

- Use the mouse effectively as the appearance and function of the mouse pointer changes

- Type and edit text in an app

- Cut or copy text and then paste it into another location

- Save files or copies of files on OneDrive

In this chapter, you will explore two apps: a picture drawing and editing program called Paint and an online word-processing program called Word Online. As you use these very different programs, you will learn about the similarities and differences between their program controls, including menus, toolbars, Ribbons, mouse pointers, and scroll bars. You also will learn widely used computer skills and program concepts, including typing and editing text on a computer; cutting, copying, and pasting text; and saving your creations online on Microsoft OneDrive. Keep in mind as you work through this chapter that while some of the skills and features are unique to these programs, many are also part of the standard features found in other Windows programs.

Learning Resources: **labyrinthelab.com/wtcb10**

📂 Case Study: Creating a Letter Including a Map

Sylvia wants to start a small home-based business. Her hobby for years has been raising goldfish. She thinks there is an untapped market in her area for setting up small aquariums in offices and providing aquarium maintenance services. To test the market, Sylvia wants to send letters and deliver fliers to local businesses explaining the products and services her business provides. She needs a small map to add to the letters, but like many small startup businesses, she doesn't have a lot of money. She decides to use the Map app that comes with Windows 10 along with the built-in snipping tool to take screen captures. She types her letters in Word Online and is then able to copy the map and paste it into her letters.

Maps, a mapping program, and Word Online, a word-processing program.

App Commands

Within apps, commands have traditionally been accessed from a series of drop-down menus on a menu bar or command buttons on a toolbar. With Office 2007, Microsoft introduced the "Windows Ribbon framework" in some of its programs as a new way to display commands, and most apps now use the **Ribbon** feature.

Menu Commands

Drop-down menus are featured in older Windows-based programs, such as Notepad. Menus are lists of commands traditionally organized in a series along a menu bar under the title bar. The first menu on most menu bars is the File menu, the second is the Edit menu, and the last is the Help menu.

Apps that use the Ribbon system to display commands do not use drop-down menus. Instead, commands are organized into tabs that open in the Ribbon. The File menu may still use a drop-down menu or open a completely new screen called a program stage depending on the app and the amount of information that needs to be displayed.

Ribbon with Home tab showing

Many of the commands in Notepad's File menu are standard to most programs, including Word Online. On the other hand, File Explorer (a file-management app) has commands related to managing files and folders that do not appear in the menus of Notepad or Word Online.

Tip! Menu commands do not always appear in the same order in different programs, and the text labels can vary.

🖱 HANDS-ON 4.1 Compare Drop-Down Menus

In this exercise, you will launch Notepad and Paint. You will compare common features in the File and Edit drop-down menus in these programs.

1. Open the **Start** ⊞ menu and choose **All Apps→Windows Accessories→Notepad**.

2. Repeat step 1, but this time launch **Paint**.

3. Use the taskbar to make **Notepad** the active program window.

4. Follow the steps below to access the File drop-down menu:

Ⓐ Click **File** on the menu bar to access the menu.

Ⓑ Taking care not to click anything, run your mouse pointer over the commands to momentarily highlight each one.

Ⓒ Dismiss the menu by clicking in a clear area outside the menu but within the **Notepad** window.

5. Make **Paint** the active program and then repeat step 3 with the Paint menu to see how it is similar to and different from Notepad's File menu.
   Notice that the menus have common features, including New, Open, Save, Save As, Print, and Exit.

6. Compare Notepad's traditional Edit menu with Paint's new Home tab, which holds the Cut, Copy, and Paste commands.

7. Click **Close** ✕ to exit Notepad, but leave Paint open.

· ·

Commands in Programs with Ribbons

Two of the programs used in this book, Paint and Word Online, use Ribbons to display commands. These commands are divided among a number of tabs.

Both of these Ribbons have some features and tools in common, but many tools are specific to each program's function (e.g., Paint is used to create and edit pictures, and Word Online is used to create and edit text).

Quick Access Toolbar

A toolbar is used to display series of commands as small buttons or drop-down lists. Commands on a toolbar or Ribbon are often referred to as "tools." The **Quick Access toolbar** typically has three tools displayed: Save, Undo, and Redo.

The Quick Access toolbar will also have a drop-down menu that enables you to add additional commands to the toolbar.

Ribbon Tabs

Paint has only two Ribbon tabs: Home and View. Word Online and some other programs have many more tabs.

A Ribbon contains many tools. Tabs on the Ribbon are used to arrange tools by task. On each tab, related tools are assembled into command groups. Each command group has vertical separators and a label. Within each group, tools can be displayed as buttons, drop-down lists, or **galleries** of options from which to choose.

The icon for each tool attempts to indicate its purpose, but you can use your mouse pointer to hover over a tool to display its name and function in a ScreenTip.

The selected tool (the Pencil) is currently the active tool.

Pencil tool —

Eraser tool —

Pencil

Draw a free-form line with the selected line width.

When you use your mouse pointer to hover over a Ribbon tool, a ScreenTip displays the tool's name and function.

The three groups on this Ribbon tab are divided with vertical separators and labeled Tools, Brushes, and Shapes.

Tip! If you are new to computers and feel uncomfortable using a mouse, try drawing pictures and then carefully erasing lines in Paint. This is a fun and easy way to improve your mouse skills.

HANDS-ON 4.2 Draw in the Paint App

In this exercise, you will draw a face and sign your name using the Pencil tool in Paint.

1. Follow these steps to use the Pencil tool:

Ⓐ Click the **Home** tab.

Ⓑ Click once on the **Pencil** tool to select it.

Ⓒ Point with the mouse pointer over the white canvas in the drawing area. The mouse pointer will now look like a pencil.

Ⓓ Drag (hold down the left mouse button and move) the Pencil in a circle to draw a rough circle for a face. Release the mouse button once you've drawn the circle.

Ⓔ Drag the Pencil to draw other parts of the face. Release the mouse button after completing each part.

Ⓕ Try signing your name by dragging using the Pencil.

You will save your work in the next exercise.

Note! If you don't like what you've drawn, choose the Eraser tool from the Tools group, drag to erase, and then choose the Pencil to try again.

Saving Your Work

When you type a letter or create a drawing as you did in the previous exercise, you usually want to save it so you can look at or work on it again later, but the computer does not save your work unless you command it to do so. Remember that if you save it to OneDrive, you can view it on any machine or device.

This section looks at two commands used to save your work: Save and Save As.

Tip! Saving your work frequently also protects you from any sudden computer failure or loss of power.

Where Your Work Is Located

In Chapter 1, Getting Your First Look, you learned that all of the things displayed on your screen are temporarily stored in the RAM chips of the computer. The work you have done so far in Paint is only temporarily stored in RAM, and if the power were to go out or someone were to shut down the computer, your work would be lost.

You must therefore save your work on a permanent storage device, such as a hard drive or a USB flash drive, or online to OneDrive to keep it from being erased. See Behind the Screen: Drive Designations on page 158 for descriptions of storage devices.

Windows needs to know two things the first time you save your work:

- What do you want to call it?

- Where do you want to store it?

Files and Folders

These two basic terms, files and folders, will be covered in more detail in Chapter 6, Finding Files, but they need to be defined here:

- **File**—A collection of data stored with a name. Examples of files are a letter you've typed and saved, a drawing in Paint that you've saved, or a picture copied from the Internet.

- **Folder**—An electronic location in which you store related groups of files. For example, Pictures and Documents are folders already created for your username in Windows in which you can store photos and other files.

Choosing a Storage Location

Today's computers provide a variety of storage options, including internal and external hard drives, DVDs, USB flash drives, and online locations, like OneDrive, Google Drive, and others, which you were introduced to in Chapter 3, Creating an Online Account. When you are ready to save, you choose which storage device you want to use. And remember, if you don't choose, the computer will choose for you (using what is called a *default* setting).

The Internal Hard Drive

When saving your work (file) for the first time, most Windows programs will direct you to a predetermined location (folder) on the internal hard drive. On your home computer:

- Notepad directs you to the Documents folder.

- Paint directs you to the Pictures folder.

Using the predetermined location is usually appropriate for new users until they learn more about the Windows storage system, which is covered in Chapter 6, Finding Files.

A Portable USB Flash Drive

You can choose a different location for saving from the one chosen by a program. In most computer labs, students save their work on USB flash drives (also called thumb, pen, or keychain drives). This storage method makes it easy to access files on your home computer as well. A flash drive is a device with a USB plug attached to a storage card. The flash drive can be plugged into any USB port on a computer.

Connecting a flash drive to a computer

OneDrive

You can choose to save your files to OneDrive (your cloud storage), which is just as easy to do as saving your work to your USB flash drive. By saving online, your files are accessible on any computer or device with an Internet connection and browser. This is the preferred method when using this book and is the one shown in most exercises.

Filenames

Data that is stored on a storage device is called a file. A file might contain a text document, a picture, a song, a movie, or any other kind of data. The first time you store data, it must be given a filename. The filename must follow Windows' file-naming conventions (rules).

NAMING FILES

Convention	Description
Filename length	Up to 255 characters
Allowed characters	All alphanumeric characters except those that are reserved (see below)
Reserved characters	| \ ? * < " : > /
Reserved words	CON, PRN, AUX, NUL, COM1 (2-9), LPT1 (2-9)

Tip! Choose a filename that will help you recognize the file's contents months from now. A filename like *Sales Letter to Business Offices* is more useful than *Sales Letter*. If possible, keep the length less than 20 characters or so to make the name easier to read in various windows and dialog boxes.

Save Versus Save As

The first time you save a document with the Save command, Windows opens a Save As dialog box asking for a filename and a storage location. After a file has been saved, choosing the Save command will save the changes without opening a dialog box, because Windows already knows the filename and location.

The Save As command is also used to save a copy of a file in three ways:

- It lets you save an existing file with a different name (leaving the original file intact).

- It lets you save an existing file to another location (the filename can be the same or different).

- It lets you save an existing file in a different format, like PDF.

HANDS-ON 4.3 Save a New Document

Saving protects your work from a power failure or other loss. In this exercise, you will save your Paint picture to your hard drive, your USB flash drive, and to OneDrive. While you normally will save to just one storage location, here you are practicing saving to multiple locations.

Before You Begin: Paint should still be open.

1. Make **Paint** the active program window.

2. Click the **File** tab and choose **Save**.

Paint opens a Save As dialog box the first time a document is saved. Notice that Paint directs you to a folder (in this example, Pictures) and has provided a temporary filename, Untitled.

Pictures is the default folder chosen by Paint.

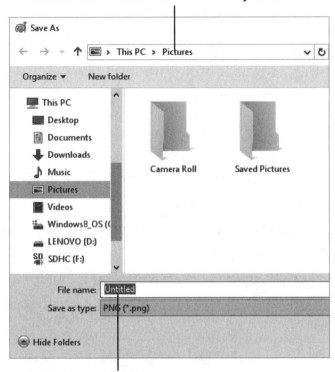

Paint also proposes an initial filename for the unsaved picture.

In the next step, you will choose a storage location for your file. Your instructor will give you guidance on where to store your file.

Save to the Hard Drive

In steps 3–5, you will practice saving the file to three different storage locations. Normally you will save to just one location.

Follow these steps to save your file to the Pictures folder:

Ⓐ If necessary, double-click the default filename to select it, and then type
My Signature.

Ⓑ Click **Save**.

Paint saves your file to the hard drive. The new filename, My Signature, is displayed on the title bar.

Save to a USB Flash Drive

3. Choose **File** → **Save As**.

4. Follow these steps to save your file to a USB flash drive:

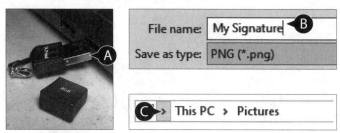

A Place your USB flash drive into a USB port on the front or back of the computer, or perhaps into a cable. Ask for help, if necessary.

B If necessary, double-click the default filename to select it, and then type **My Signature**.

C Click the first drop-down list ▾ button on the address bar to open the menu.

Drop-down list buttons often show a right-pointing arrow ▶ that, when clicked, becomes a downward-pointing arrow ▾.

D Choose **This PC**.

E Click the second drop-down list ▾ button and choose your USB flash drive (the drive name/letter will likely differ from what's shown).

F Click **Save** or tap Enter .

A copy of My Signature is saved on your flash drive.

My Signature - Paint

Save to OneDrive

5. Choose **File→Save As**.

6. Follow these steps to save your file to OneDrive:

Ⓐ If necessary, double-click the default filename to select it and then type
   My Signature.

Ⓑ Click the first drop-down list ▼ button on the address bar to open the menu.

Ⓒ Choose **OneDrive**, and then click **Save** or tap ⃞Enter⃞.

Ⓓ Click **Save** or tap ⃞Enter⃞ on the keyboard.

*A copy of My Signature is saved on OneDrive. You now have three copies of the file, each
saved to a different storage location.*

6. Close **Paint**.

The Work Area

Up to this point, you have concentrated on features on the perimeter of program
windows, such as borders, menus, and control buttons. These are the tools that help
when you are working in a program. Now you will look more closely at the work area,
the place where you use the tools and do the work.

Mouse Pointers

In the last exercise, you saw that the mouse pointer looked like a pencil when the
Pencil tool was active. In Windows, the appearance of the mouse pointer changes as
the functions or capabilities of the mouse pointer change.

WINDOWS MOUSE POINTERS

Mouse Pointer	Function
⌖	Normal selection pointer
I	Text selection pointer
⊹	Precision selection pointer
✥	Move pointer
↔	Horizontal resize pointer
↕	Vertical resize pointer

Tool Galleries

Many tool groups in Paint include galleries, which are collections of tools or options. Tools in a gallery may be shown in full or partial view, or they may be hidden from view as a button on the Ribbon. If only part of the gallery is visible, a scroll bar is provided to view the remaining tools. If a gallery is hidden, its gallery button will display a downward-pointing arrow, which must be **selected** in order to display its drop-down gallery.

Tip! Users new to a program with a Ribbon will find it easier to use the Ribbon if the program window is maximized. Some tool groups and galleries change to buttons as the window is made smaller.

Paint will remember the most recently selected options the next time you use that tool. Also, be aware that when different tools are selected, options such as line thickness in the Size gallery can change.

The line thickness options available in the Size gallery when Pencil is the active tool.

Airbrush is the selected tool in this drop-down Brushes gallery.

The size options are different when Airbrush is made the active tool.

HANDS-ON 4.4 Change Mouse Pointers in Paint

In this exercise, you will select different tools from the Paint program Ribbon and observe appearance changes in the mouse pointer as you create a drawing.

1. Choose **Start** ▦ →**All Apps**→**Windows Accessories**→**Paint**.

2. **Maximize** ▭ the window and then click the **Home** tab.

3. Click the buttons in the Tools group one at a time and move your mouse over the white canvas to see the mouse pointer.
   Notice the changing appearance of the mouse pointer.

4. Follow these step-by-step options for the Rectangle tool:

Ⓐ Choose the **Rectangle** tool from the Shapes gallery.

Ⓑ Click the **Outline** tool and choose the **Solid Color** option.

Ⓒ Click the **Fill** tool and choose **Solid Color**.

Ⓓ Click the **Color 2** tool and choose **Gray–25%** from the color palette.

5. Point near the top of the drawing area and then drag down and to the right to make a box.

The line color is determined by the Color 1 choice; the fill color is determined by the Color 2 choice.

6. Follow these steps to set up and use the Eraser tool:

Ⓐ Choose the **Eraser** tool.

Ⓑ Pick any size for the eraser from the Size gallery.

Ⓒ Click **Color 2** and choose **White** as the background color.

Ⓓ Drag with the **Eraser** tool to erase part of the box.

Notice that the mouse pointer changes to reflect the size and color of the Eraser. The Eraser tool does not actually erase; rather, it paints using what you chose as Color 2.

7. Leave Paint open for the next exercise.

Scroll Bars

When part of your picture or content is too large be seen in the app window, Windows will display scroll bars. A vertical scroll bar will let you move up or down, and a horizontal scroll bar will let you move side to side. In some apps, the scroll bars don't appear until you move your mouse toward the bottom or right side of the app window.

Each scroll bar has three parts:

HANDS-ON 4.5 Use Scroll Bars

In this exercise, you will resize the Paint window and use the vertical and horizontal scroll bars.

Before You Begin: Resize the Paint window so scroll bars appear.

1. Restore down ⬜ the Paint window. Click the edge of the program window until you see vertical and horizontal scroll bars.

2. Follow these steps to practice scrolling up and down:

Ⓐ Point at the scroll box, hold down the mouse button, and drag it downward about an inch.

Ⓑ Click several times on the down scroll button to scroll down farther.

Ⓒ Click several times on the up scroll button to scroll back to the top.

Ⓓ Click once on the scroll bar to jump farther down than you would by scrolling.

3. Try using parts of the horizontal scroll bar to scroll from side to side.

4. Close **Paint**. Do not save the file.

Typing with Word Online

Word Online is a free and basic word-processing program from Microsoft that is used to type letters and other simple documents. Although it is a basic app, it makes an excellent learning program because it has many features common to other online and desktop applications.

Word Online Ribbon

Like the Paint program, Word Online uses a Ribbon instead of the traditional system of a menu bar and toolbars. Many of the features in Word Online's Ribbon are like those found in Microsoft Word 2013 and 2016.

Tabs

The Word Online Ribbon contains multiple tabs. On each tab, tools with a related function are assembled into command groups, which are further divided by vertical separators and labeled.

Drop-Down Lists

Word Online has several drop-down lists on the Home tab that are represented and accessed by clicking a button containing a downward-pointing arrow. Three frequently used drop-down lists are located in the Font group: Font Name, Font Size, and Font Color. Some drop-down lists (such as Font Name) are quite long and include a scroll bar.

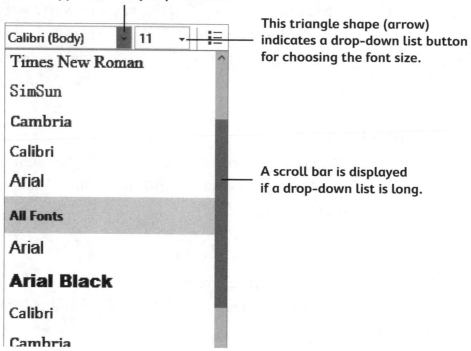

This is how a drop-down list button appears when you point at it.

This triangle shape (arrow) indicates a drop-down list button for choosing the font size.

A scroll bar is displayed if a drop-down list is long.

ScreenTips

Just as you saw in Paint, when you rest your mouse pointer over a tool or drop-down list in the Ribbon in Word Online, a ScreenTip helps you determine its name and function.

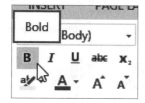

Tip! When you discover a useful feature such as ScreenTips in one program, check to see if the same feature is used in other programs.

The Cursor and the Mouse Pointer

Users who are new to word-processing programs such as Word Online can be confused by what appears to be two cursors: One is the blinking **cursor** in the text, and the other is the *mouse pointer* (which can appear almost everywhere you point). The blinking cursor is often also called the **insertion point**. When you type, the text is inserted to the left of the blinking cursor.

When you type, text goes in front of the blinking cursor|

The blinking cursor

The mouse pointer, which looks like an I-beam when in a text area

When Word Online is first opened, the blinking cursor is located at the top of the white writing area. This white writing area is equivalent to a sheet of paper.

Tip! Most of the word-processing skills learned in this chapter can be used to type email and work in most other word-processing programs.

Special Keys on the Keyboard

Computer keyboards have keys that perform tasks that are particular to working with apps. This section discusses some of the most popular ones, and in the next exercise, you'll use these keys and more.

Backspace and Delete Keys

The Backspace key on the keyboard erases text to the left of the cursor. The Delete key erases text to the right of the cursor.

The Backspace key erases text to the left of the cursor.

The Delete key erases text to the right of the cursor.

Tab Key

The Tab key moves the cursor right to the next half-inch mark on the ruler. This is a useful key for creating accurately aligned columns.

Some apps, like Word Online, don't support the Tab key function. Companies make choices about what features they are going to support in the free versions of their programs.

Enter Key

The [Enter] key has two functions: It ends a paragraph, and it moves any text below or to the right of the cursor down two lines. Holding the [Shift] key and tapping [Enter] moves the cursor down one line.

🖱 HANDS-ON 4.6 Type in Word Online

In this exercise, you will do basic typing using the [Spacebar] and [Enter] keys; correct mistakes using [Backspace] and [Delete]; and move around using the [Home], [End], and arrow keys.

Before You Begin: Log in to OneDrive using the instructions from Chapter 3: Creating an Online Account.

1. Click the **app launcher** on the left-side of the OneDrive title bar, and then click **Word Online** on the menu that appears.

2. Choose **New Blank Document**.

3. **Maximize** [□] the browser window.

4. Type the following:

   To: [Spacebar] Emily [Spacebar] Carlito [Shift] + [Enter] From: [Spacebar] Dan [Spacebar] Lewis [Enter] Dear [Spacebar] Emily,

   Notice that using the [Spacebar] puts a space between words. When [Shift]+[Enter] is typed, it ends a paragraph and moves the cursor down one line. When the [Enter] key is typed by itself, it ends the paragraph and moves the cursor down two lines.

5. Tap [Enter] to create two new lines and then type the following:

   If I type a sentence that is too long to fit on one line, I do not have to tap the Enter key when I get near the margin because the words will automatically wrap to a new line. [Enter]

   Typing is fun.

   Most word-processing and email programs automatically wrap text. It is necessary to tap [Enter] only when you want to end a paragraph and force text to start on a new line.
   Leave Word Online open.

Editing Text

Word processing enables you to extensively edit and format the text before it is printed. When you are typing text, concentrate on getting your ideas typed first and worry about spelling, grammar, and layout later.

Tip! When typing a letter, report, or story, you do not have to stop and make corrections as you type. You can always make corrections later. If you stop to correct errors, you break your train of thought and may forget some important ideas.

Selecting Text

Text is *selected* before it can be edited (changed). Selecting text lets the computer know which part of the text to change. When text is selected, it typically becomes highlighted as though it is marked with a highlighter pen.

Word Online highlights selected text.

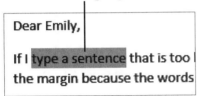

There may be more than one way to select the same text, and you will become more productive if you become familiar with the different selection methods.

SELECTING TEXT

Selection Procedure	Result
Drag with mouse	Selects a letter, word, sentence, or paragraph
Double-click	Selects a word
Triple-click	Selects an entire paragraph

FROM THE KEYBOARD

Ctrl + A to select an entire document

HANDS-ON 4.7 Select Text

In this exercise, you will select text by dragging and clicking with the mouse.

Before You Begin: Word Online should still be open.

1. Follow these steps to select text:

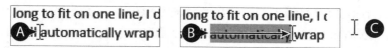

Ⓐ Put the mouse pointer in front of the word *automatically*.

Ⓑ Drag to the end of the word and then release the mouse button. Word Online highlights the word you selected.

Ⓒ Click somewhere else to deselect (turn off) the highlighted word.

2. Place the mouse pointer over the word *automatically* and double-click.

   Word Online selects the entire word and the space after the word. This is a bit easier than dragging to select the single word.

3. Click away from the word to deselect it.

4. Drag the mouse pointer over the entire first paragraph to select it and then click away from it to deselect it.

5. Point the mouse pointer over the first paragraph and triple-click to select it; click away from it to deselect it.

   When you triple-click, you do not have to click rapidly. Just click three times smoothly without moving the mouse. Word Online selects the entire paragraph.

Save Your Work

When you finish a significant piece of work on a document, it's always a good idea to save it.

6. Choose **File→Save As**.

   Word Online displays the various save options.

7. Choose the **Save As** button to save a copy to OneDrive.

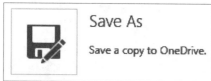

8. In the dialog box that appears, click the **Save** button to save in the default OneDrive location.

   In Chapter 7, Storing Files, you will learn more about creating folders for saving and organizing your files.

9. Type the new filename **Memo to Emily Carlito** and click **Save**.

   Your document is now saved to OneDrive. Notice that the name of your document is now in the title bar for Word Online.

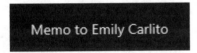

10. Leave Word Online open.

Formatting Text

Another editing task you can perform is text formatting. Formatting text in Word Online includes choosing a text style (Font Name), text size (Font Size, Grow Font, or Shrink Font), text style (**Bold**, *Italic*, <u>Underline</u>), and text color (Font Color). These button or drop-down list choices can be found on the Home tab in the Font group.

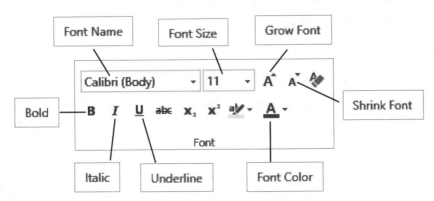

The Font group on the Home tab in Word Online

Note! Remember, you must select the text you want to format *before* you choose any formatting changes.

HANDS-ON 4.8 Format Text

In this exercise, you will change formatting using various buttons and drop-down lists.

Before You Begin: Word Online should still be open.

1. Follow these steps to make formatting changes to the text you have typed:

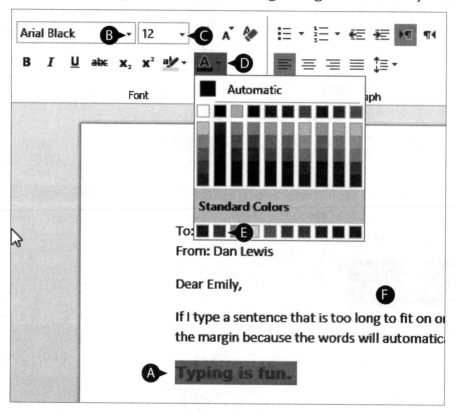

Ⓐ Drag or triple-click to select the last paragraph (make sure this text stays selected as you perform steps B–E).

Ⓑ Click the **Font Name** list ▾ button and choose **Arial Black**.

Ⓒ Click the **Font Size** list ▾ button and choose **12**.

Ⓓ Click the **Font Color** list ▾ button.

Ⓔ Choose any text color.

Ⓕ Click once on a clear area to deselect the text.

As you can see, as long as the text remains selected, you can repeatedly apply formatting commands to it.

2. Follow these steps to format a single word.

Ⓐ Double-click on the word *Carlito* to select it.

Ⓑ Change the style to **Bold**.

Ⓒ Change the color to **Blue**.

Ⓓ Click on a clear area to deselect the word.

It's easy to select and format single words.

3. Leave Word Online open.

Printing a Document

You may want to print a drawing or letter you have created. Most apps provide three commands to help you print:

- **Print Preview**—Preview the document on the monitor and make changes before you print.

- **Quick Print**—Send the document directly to the printer without any changes.

- **Print**—Select the printer, pages to print, number of copies, and other options before printing.

Print commands can be accessed on the File menu and sometimes via buttons on a toolbar.

Online Apps

Because of the way online apps are designed, your document has to be converted into a printable form. This is usually done by converting it into a PDF file (see Saving a File as a PDF) or some other format and displaying it in a separate printing window.

Word Online

Word Online creates a temporary PDF file that then can be printed using the print function of your browser. Once printed, the browser tab is closed and the temporary PDF file is deleted.

FROM THE KEYBOARD

Ctrl + P to start the print process in most apps

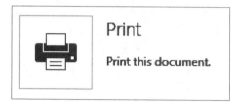 HANDS-ON 4.9 Print a Word Online Document

In this exercise, you will print the Memo to Emily Carlito.

Before You Begin: Word Online should still be open.

1. Choose **File→Print**.

2. Click the **Print** button.

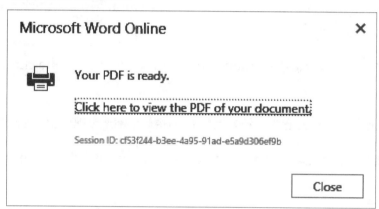

Word Online will take a few moments to generate a temporary PDF of your document.

3. In the dialog box that appears, click the link titled **Click Here to View the PDF of Your Document**.

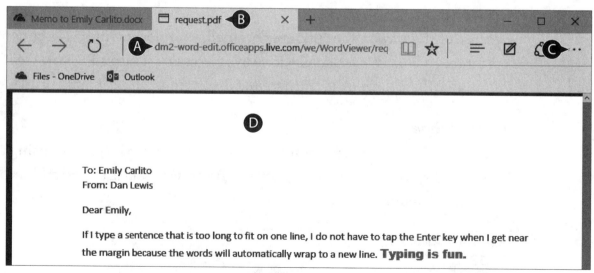

The temporary PDF of your document is opened in a separate tab in your browser.

4. Look carefully at your browser window.

Ⓐ Click the **Word Online** tab.

Ⓑ Click the temporary PDF tab.

Ⓒ Click the **More Actions** button.

Ⓓ Notice that there are no formatting controls available in the PDF tab.

5. Click the **More Actions** ⋯ button on the right-hand side of the menu bar and choose **Print** from the menu.

6. In the print dialog box make sure the correct printer is selected and the number of copies is set to **1**. Click the **Print** button.

7. **Close** ✕ the PDF tab and return to the Word Online tab.

8. **Close** ✕ the dialog box in Word Online and leave the program open.

. . . .

Saving as a PDF File

PDF is short for portable document format. PDF files store a document exactly as it was created, with all of its layout, text, and graphics intact.

PDF files are a popular way to share documents as they are machine and software independent, meaning that you don't need a specific piece of software or device to read the file. Many programs and devices can read PDF files, so the format has become a standard for sharing documents.

Many programs allow you to save your work as a PDF file. This is usually done in one of two ways: Printing to a PDF or using the Save As function to save as a PDF. Printing as a PDF means you print to a PDF "printer" instead of to your default printer.

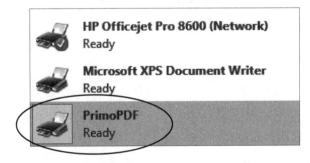

Example of a PDF "printer"

Instead of printing to paper, your document is saved to a PDF. During the process, you are given a chance to name the PDF file.

Note! Some programs have you use the Save As function to save a copy of your document as a different file type.

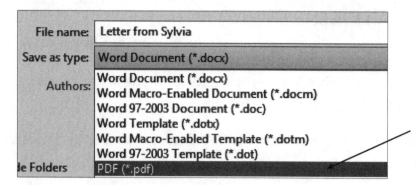

During the saving process, while naming the file, you can choose to save your document in PDF format. Online apps, like Word Online, may have slightly different ways for saving a document as a PDF.

HANDS-ON 4.10 Save a PDF File in Word Online

In this exercise, you will save a copy of your Memo to Emily Carlito as a PDF.

1. Choose **File→Save As**.

2. Click the **Download as PDF** button.

   Word Online converts a copy of your document into a temporary PDF file.

   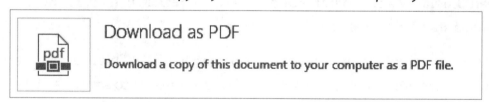

3. In the dialog box that appears, click the link **Click Here to View the PDF of Your Document**.

   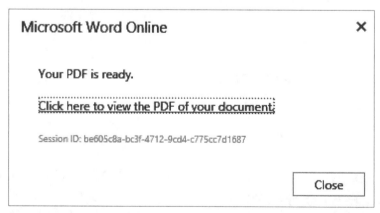

   The PDF is downloaded to the default download location for the Microsoft Edge browser. (More information on file locations and downloads can be found in later chapters.)

4. **Close** ☒ the downloading dialog at the bottom of the screen.

| Memo to Emily Carlito.pdf finished downloading. | Open | View downloads | ☒ |

5. In **Word Online**, close the dialog box regarding your PDF being ready.

   Leave Word Online open.

· ·

Cut, Copy, and Paste

Most Windows apps support the Cut, Copy, and Paste commands. In Word Online these commands are located in the Clipboard group on the Home tab.

CUT, COPY, AND PASTE COMMANDS

Command	Performs
Cut	Deletes a selected object from its present location and places a copy of the object in a special folder called Clipboard.
Copy	Places a copy of a selected object in Clipboard without deleting it from its present location.
Paste	Inserts a copy of the last object cut or copied into the present location of the cursor.
Cut and Paste	Used together, they let you move text and other objects from one place in a program to another place within the same program (or to another program).
Copy and Paste	Used together, they let you copy text or another object from one place in a program to another place within the same program (or to another program).

Tip! In some apps you can move (cut and paste) selected text by dragging and dropping it to a new location. You can make a copy of text that has been selected to paste elsewhere by dragging and dropping the selected text to the new location while holding down the ⌜Ctrl⌟ key.

QUICK REFERENCE: Using Cut or Copy and Paste Commands

Task	Procedure
Use Cut or Copy and Paste	▪ Select the text or object you want to move or copy.
	▪ Choose Home tab→Cut or Home tab→Copy.
	▪ Place the cursor where you want to paste the text or object.
	▪ Choose Home tab→Paste.
	▪ You can paste the text or object again by repeating the preceding two steps.

Keyboard Shortcuts

Some apps, especially browser-based apps, can't use the Cut, Copy, and Paste buttons because of design issues with the browser and the apps.

Use shortcut keys ✕

Your browser can't access the clipboard, so use these shortcuts:

Cut = Ctrl + X
Copy = Ctrl + C
Paste = Ctrl + V

Session ID: 5239e8b7-8b18-4e0e-957b-5909b97ccbd7

OK

You will see a message like this when required to use keyboard shortcuts.

You can still cut, copy, and paste, but you will have to use the keyboard shortcuts.

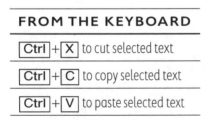

FROM THE KEYBOARD

Ctrl + X to cut selected text

Ctrl + C to copy selected text

Ctrl + V to paste selected text

Advanced Cut, Copy, and Paste

The ability to copy objects from one program to another is a powerful tool. As your skills with the computer increase, you will find that you can copy more than just text from one app to another. For example, you can do the following:

- copy text and images from the Internet into your research paper (don't forget to cite your sources!)

- copy a chart from a spreadsheet into your report

- copy information from your notes into your presentation

- copy a chart from a spreadsheet into an assignment

The general rule to follow is if you can select an item, you can probably copy and paste it.

HANDS-ON 4.11 Use Cut and Paste

In this exercise, you will cut and paste text and move it within a Word Online document. Use keyboard shortcuts if needed.

Before You Begin: Word Online should still be open to your typed document from the last exercise.

1. Follow these steps to move a paragraph using Cut and Paste:

Ⓐ Drag or triple-click to select the last paragraph.

Ⓑ Click the **Home** tab.

Ⓒ Choose **Cut**.

Word Online cuts the text and places it in the Clipboard, and the text disappears from the document. Now that the text is in the Clipboard, you can paste it to a new location.

2. Click once at the end of the last sentence to place the blinking cursor there.

> If I type a sentence that is too long to fit on one line, I do not have to tap the Enter key when I get near the margin because the words will automatically wrap to a new line.

Placing the cursor in the document tells Word Online where you want your next command (Paste) to be performed.

3. Choose **Home→Paste**.

Word Online pastes the text from the Clipboard back into the document.

4. Tap ⌈Enter⌉ and then choose **Home →Paste** from the Ribbon again.

Word Online pastes the text again. Whatever you cut or copy to the Clipboard remains there until you cut or copy something else, so you can paste the same item repeatedly if you wish.

> If I type a sentence that is too long to fit on one line, I do not have to tap the Enter key when I get near the margin because the words will automatically wrap to a new line. **Typing is fun.**
>
> **Typing is fun.**

5. Choose **Undo** from the Ribbon.

Word Online undoes your most recent command, which in this case is Paste.

6. Close the **Edge** browser. Your work is saved automatically.

Closing the browser will close the Word Online tab.

· ·

Concepts Review

To check your knowledge of the key concepts introduced in this chapter, complete the Concepts Review quiz on this page. Or, you can take the quiz online by going to **labyrinthelab/wtcb10**.

Page number

1. Cut and Paste commands let you move selections from one place to another.　　**true　false**　_____

2. A flash drive can be plugged into any USB port on a PC.　　**true　false**　_____

3. When typing text, new text is inserted in front of the I-beam mouse pointer and not in front of the blinking cursor.　　**true　false**　_____

4. Saving a file takes it from RAM and places a copy onto a drive.　　**true　false**　_____

5. "My current letter-22" is a valid filename.　　**true　false**　_____

6. The Backspace key moves the cursor to the left without erasing text.　　**true　false**　_____

7. Which command reverses your most recent task?

   a. Undo

   b. Cut

   c. Paste

   d. Save

   Page number: _____

8. The feature on the side and bottom of a program window that enables you to view a large picture or file is the _____.

   a. elevator bar

   b. scroll bar

   c. zoom bar

   d. view bar

   Page number: _____

9. Before you save your work in a program for the first time, where is it being saved temporarily?

   a. on the hard drive

   b. on the USB flash drive

   c. in RAM

   d. in the monitor

   Page number: _____

10. Use the Save As command to _____.

   a. save a copy of a file to different location

   b. save a copy of a file with a different name

   c. save an unsaved file with a name and to a location of your choosing

   d. All of the above

   Page number: _____

Skill Builders

SKILL BUILDER 4.1 **Create and Save a Letter from Start to Finish**

In this exercise, you will create, edit, and format a letter for Sylvia to use in her goldfish aquarium business and save it to OneDrive.

1. Log in to **OneDrive** and start **Word Online**.

2. Open a **New Blank Document**.

3. **Maximize** ☐ the **Edge** window.

4. Type this letter. You can use ⌷Backspace⌷ and ⌷Delete⌷ to correct errors as you type or wait until you are finished to select mistyped words and replace them.

   `Dear Business Owner,`⌷Enter⌷

   `Thank you for your interest in having an aquarium placed in your main lobby. I have enclosed a price list for the aquariums I have available. All prices include initial setup of the aquarium, the first group of goldfish, and appropriate aquatic plants.`⌷Enter⌷

   `Unless you have qualified staff to maintain the aquarium, I recommend our affordable monthly service. Our service is guaranteed.`⌷Enter⌷

   `I will arrange an appointment next week to review the details.`⌷Enter⌷

   `Sincerely,`⌷Enter⌷

   `Sylvia Tiger-Shark`⌷SHIFT⌷+⌷Enter⌷
   `Owner`⌷SHIFT⌷+⌷Enter⌷

   `Living Office`⌷Enter⌷

Edit the Letter

5. If you have not done so already, select any errors and replace them with corrected text.

6. Press ⌷Ctrl⌷+⌷A⌷ to select all text in the document.

7. Use the **Font Size** to change the font size to **12 pt**.

8. Click once somewhere in the document to deselect the text.

9. Select the words *Living Office* on the last line and make them **Bold**.

Save the Letter

10. Choose **File→Save As** and then click the **Save As** button.

11. In the OneDrive dialog box, click **Save** to save your file to the default location.

12. Type the filename **Letter from Sylvia** and click **Save**.
Leave Word Online open for next exercise.

. . . .

SKILL BUILDER 4.2 Create a Copy of Your Letter

In this exercise, you will create a copy of Letter from Sylvia from the last lesson and address it to a specific person.

1. In **Word Online**, choose **File→New**.

2. Open a new **Blank Document**.

3. Click on the browser tab for the **Letter from Sylvia**.

4. Press Ctrl+A to select the entire letter.

5. Press Ctrl+C to copy the letter to the Clipboard.

6. Click the browser tab named for the blank document you created.

7. Press Ctrl+V to paste the letter into the document.

8. Delete the text *Business Owner* and replace with the text **Office Manager**.

> Dear Office Manager,
>
> Thank you for your interest in havin
> for the aquariums I have available.
> goldfish, and appropriate aquatic pl

9. Save the file to the **OneDrive** default location with the name **Office Manager Letter**.

Save as a PDF

10. Choose **File** → **Save As** and then choose **Download as PDF**.

11. View the PDF and then close the download bar.

Letter from Sylvia.pdf finished downloading.   Open   Open folder   View downloads   ✕

12. Close the **Word Online** dialog box.

13. Close **Edge**.

CHAPTER 5

Using Email

LEARNING OBJECTIVES

- Create a properly formatted email address
- Send and receive emails, including those with attachments
- Create folders and organize emails using Outlook.com
- Identify spam and other email threats

In this chapter, you will learn about email and how email addresses are formatted. As you progress through the chapter, you will learn how to use the Outlook.com app to send, receive, and organize your email as well as to learn about security tips to protect against threats that come through email.

📂 Case Study: Time for Email

Jodi has a problem. She recently enrolled in college, and everyone wants her email address. She doesn't have one and is not sure how to get started. Up to this point, she has gotten by with just her phone.

Jodi talks with her friend Nadia, who explains that she can get a free email address from Microsoft and then shows Jodi how to use Outlook.com to send and receive emails. Nadia also explains how Jodi can use any device, including her smartphone, to send and receive emails. Before long, Jodi is spending as much time emailing on her laptop as she does talking on her phone!

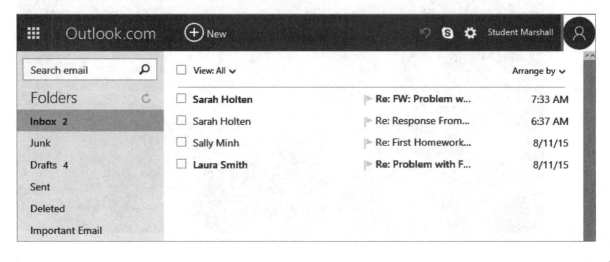

What Is Email?

Email (short for "electronic mail") was first created in 1971 when Ray Tomlinson, an early Internet pioneer, was tasked with finding something interesting to do with the earliest version of the Internet. Today, an estimated 180 billion emails are sent around the world every day.

Email is an electronic message that is sent over the Internet. A message can contain text, graphics, and more. Files, called attachments, can be connected to your email message, making it a fast and efficient way to send documents and photos.

How Does Email Work?

Email works like sending a letter through the U.S. Post Office. When you send an email, you use a person's individual email address, which points to a specific electronic post office, called an email server, on the Internet. When that person checks for email, their messages are copied from the email server onto their computer, device, or smartphone.

Email Address

Your email address is like your street or PO box address; it identifies the location where people can send messages to you. Your email address is unique, and you are the only one who can have that specific email address.

yourname@domain.com

An email address is made of two pieces: a local piece and a domain piece separated by an @ (pronounced "at") symbol. The local piece is your unique name, like an individual PO box number, and the domain piece after the @ symbol defines the location of your electronic post office on the Internet.

Note! The @ symbol was chosen because of all the nonalphanumeric characters on the keyboard that didn't already have a function, it was the least likely to be confused with being part of the local name.

Outlook.com

Outlook.com is a free, web-based email service that you can use to send, receive, and organize your emails. It's a basic version of the full version app, Microsoft Outlook, which, like the full version of Microsoft Word, is available for purchase.

Outlook.com and the full version of Outlook are similar. You will find that many businesses use Outlook as their primary email program.

Other free email services exist and are widely used on the Internet. Some of the most popular include Gmail, Yahoo! Mail, and Mail.com.

Logging in to Outlook.com is very similar to logging in to Word Online. Both use the same login that you created in Chapter 3, Creating an Online Account.

HANDS-ON 5.1 Log In to Outlook.com

In this exercise, you will log in to Outlook.com for the first time. The first step is to log in to OneDrive.

1. Start **Microsoft Edge**.

2. Type **onedrive.live.com** into the address bar of the browser and press ⌸Enter⌸.

3. Sign in to **OneDrive**, if necessary.

   See Hands-On 3.3, steps 5–6, if you have any problems.

Log In to Outlook.com

4. Click the **app launcher** on the left side of the OneDrive title bar, then click **Outlook.com**.

5. Choose **Skip for Now** if it asks about adding an Outlook.com email address.

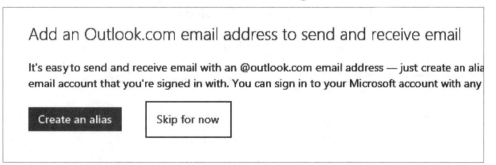

Anytime Outlook.com asks if you want to create an email address, just skip or decline. Messages will pop up on a regular basis about creating an Outlook.com email address, but since you already have an email address associated with this account, you do not need to do so.

6. Close **Outlook.com**.

The Outlook.com Screen

The Outlook.com screen is very dynamic; the screen changes to show you the commands you need at that moment. Instead of a Ribbon with multiple tabs full of commands, the app provides a menu bar containing changing commands.

For example, when you are preparing to send a new email, the menu bar changes to show you only the relevant sending commands, and a formatting menu appears.

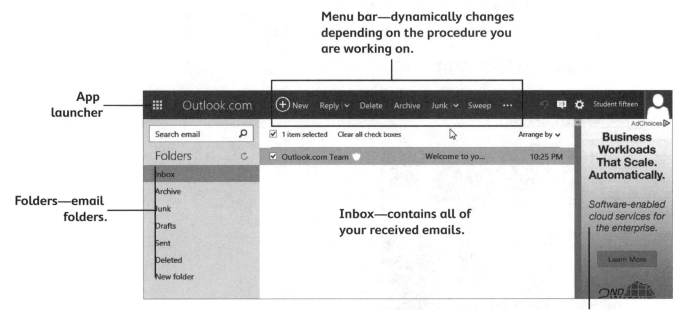

Menu bar—dynamically changes depending on the procedure you are working on.

App launcher

Folders—email folders.

Inbox—contains all of your received emails.

Advertising—Microsoft keeps Outlook.com free by including advertising that appears on the side of the screen.

The Inbox shows some basic information about the emails that have been sent to you, including the name of the sender, the subject, and the date/time it was sent. It also shows the following icons, which contain commands relating to email.

Use this to mark the message as read/unread.

Use this to keep the message at the top of the inbox.

Use this to delete the message.

Use this to read the message.

When you use your mouse pointer to hover over the subject line of an email, you are shown commands for deleting it, marking it as read/unread, or keeping it on the top of the list of emails as a priority. You can also click an email's subject line to read it.

HANDS-ON 5.2 Read an Email

In this exercise, you will open and read an email from the Outlook.com Team.
Before You Begin: Log in to OneDrive using the instructions in Hands-On 3.3.

1. Click the **app launcher** on the left side of the OneDrive title bar and then click **Outlook.com** on the menu that appears.

2. Open the email from the Outlook.com Team by clicking on its subject line.

Notice that your mouse pointer turns into a pointing finger when you are positioned in the correct area to click. When you click, your inbox shows you the message. If you have a moment, read through the email and learn about some of the things Outlook.com can do.

3. Click **Inbox** in the Folders pane to close the email and return to the Inbox.

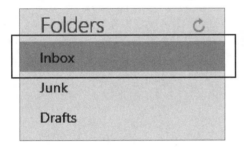

4. Close **Outlook.com**.

Sending Messages

One of the primary jobs of any email app is to facilitate the sending of messages. Starting an email message in Outlook.com is as simple as clicking the New button.

Messages include the following components:

- The recipient's email address

- A subject line (not required, but highly recommended)

- Message body text

- Attachments (optional)

Once the first three steps are completed (attaching a file is optional), your email is ready to be sent.

The various screens in Outlook.com are designed to be responsive to the potentially changing size of the program window; as the size changes, the layout of the various screens changes as well. The same commands are available, but their position on the screen may change. This is called "responsive design," and it allows a web-based app to transition between being used on laptops, devices, and smartphones.

Address line (for the recipient's email address)

Message options displayed on a menu bar

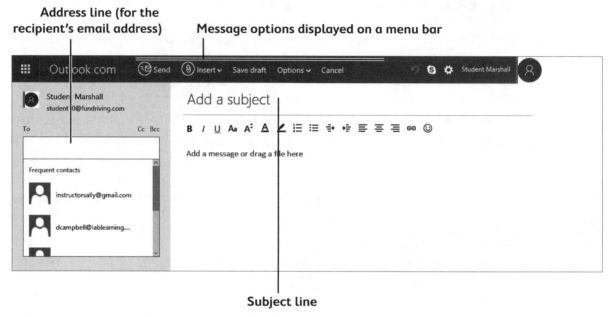

Subject line

Drafting a new email message—maximized window

Address line (for the recipient's email address)

Message options on the menu bar are condensed because of the window size.

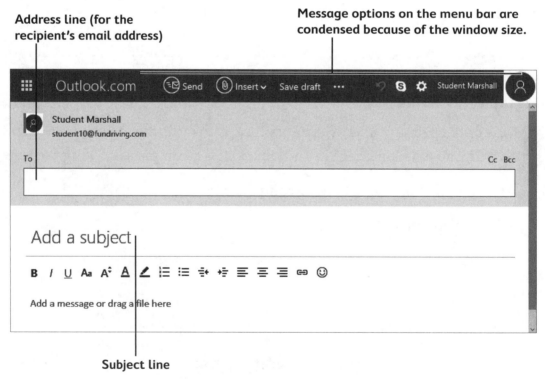

Subject line

Drafting a new email message—small screen

Message options are further condensed when using Outlook.com on a smartphone.

Compose

From: student10@fundriving.com

Address line (for the recipient's email address)

To:

Cc/Bcc:

Subject line — Subject:

Sent by Outlook for Android

Drafting a new email message—Android smartphone

Address Line

The address line (preceded by the word *To*) is where you enter a recipient's email address. It's very important to type the recipient's email address completely and exactly. If you enter an incomplete email address, the program inserts a colored box around it, and you must fix it before the email can be sent.

The incorrect address on the right should read student@labpub.com.

Multiple email addresses can be added by separating addresses with a comma.

Clicking the Cc (carbon copy) link located at the end of the address line tells the app to provide a new address line for entering other recipients who should receive a copy of the same email. Many times in business you cc someone on a message when you want to make that person aware of what is going on but don't require a response.

The Bcc (blind carbon copy) link works like carbon copy, except the recipient(s) of the email does not know that a different recipient is also receiving a copy.

An email address can be removed from a message by clicking the Close button to the right of the address.

MESSAGE ADDRESS OPTIONS

Option	Description
To	The primary address line in an email
Cc, or carbon copy	Sends a copy of the email to another recipient
Bcc, or blind carbon copy	Sends a copy of the email to another recipient without the original recipient knowing
"," (comma)	Separates multiple email addresses in the address line

Subject Line

The subject line briefly describes the email's topic, and many people consider it to be as important as the message itself. This is because many office workers get hundreds of emails a day, and they use the subject lines to help them decide which emails to read first.

Keep the subject line very short and to the point.

SUBJECT LINE EXAMPLES

Bad Subject Line	Good Subject Line
Homework	Homework assignment #4 attached
Approved	Changes to Project Approved
Need Help!	Need Help With Windows 10 Problem

Writing Your Message

Writing your message works just like typing text in Word Online. Text can be formatted with bold, italics, and underline, and the color, font, and size of text can also be changed.

You may also copy and paste text from other apps directly into the email message. This is useful for sharing quotes or other information you have found on the Internet.

HANDS-ON 5.3 Send an Email Message

In this exercise, you will send an email message.

1. Open **Outlook.com**.

2. Click the **New** button on the menu bar.

3. In the address line type **laura.smith@lablearning.net** and then click the **Cc** link to open a carbon copy address line.

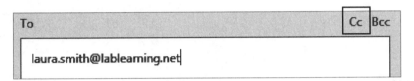

Notice a second address line opens.

4. In the Cc address line, type **dcampbell@lablearning.com** and click in the subject line.

5. In the subject line type **Problem with Free Bobble-head Offer**, and then click in the message area of the email.

6. Type the following in the message area:

To Whom It May Concern, ⌨Enter

⌨Enter **I recently registered on your website to receive a free collectible bobble-head doll. It has been six weeks, and I have not received any reply or the free doll.** ⌨Enter

⌨Enter **If possible, please let me know the status of my doll.** ⌨Enter

⌨Enter **Thank you,** ⌨Enter

Your Name

7. Click the **Send** button on the menu bar.

Your message is immediately sent, a copy is moved to the Sent folder, and you are returned to the Inbox.

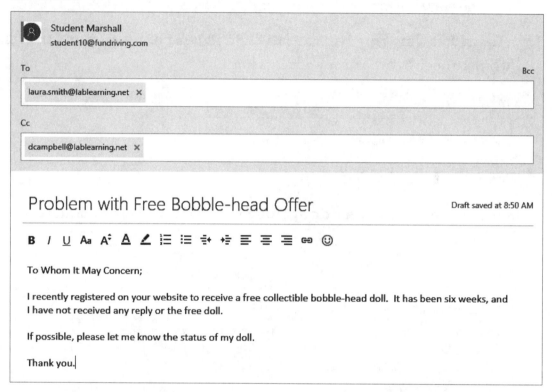

8. Close **Outlook.com**.

Attachments

Emails can have files attached that are sent with the message. You can attach almost any file type, including documents, images, recordings, and videos.

Depending on the company providing the email service, there may be limits on the types of files allowed in attachments. For example, many email providers do not let you send apps as attachments due to the security risks.

Email providers may also limit the size of the email attachments you send. This size maximum varies depending on the provider. For example, Gmail limits the size of each attachment to 25 megabytes, whereas Outlook.com limits the size of each attachment to 100 megabytes.

Tip! Even if your email provider does not limit the size of attachments, your recipient's provider may, which may mean that they won't be able to open a large attachment that you send or that the message may not be delivered.

HANDS-ON 5.4 Send an Email with an Attachment

In this exercise, you will send a file that you created in Chapter 4, Working with Apps, as an email attachment.

Before You Begin: This exercise assumes you saved the My Signature file you created in Hands-On 4.3 on your USB flash drive.

1. Open **Outlook.com**.

2. Click the **New** button on the Outlook.com menu bar.

3. In the address line type `instructorsally@gmail.com`.

4. In the subject line type `First Homework Assignment`.

5. Type the following in the message area:

   `Attached you will find homework assignment #1. Hopefully my drawing skills are up to your expectations!` Enter

   `Thank you,` Enter

   `Your Name`

6. Click **Insert** on the menu bar and then click **Files As Attachments** from the drop-down menu.

An Open dialog box will appear that will allow you to navigate to the location of the file you wish to attach.

7. Choose your USB flash drive from the navigation pane on the left and then choose the **My Signature** file from the View pane on the right.

If in Hands-On 4.3 you saved your file to a different location, choose that location from the navigation pane.

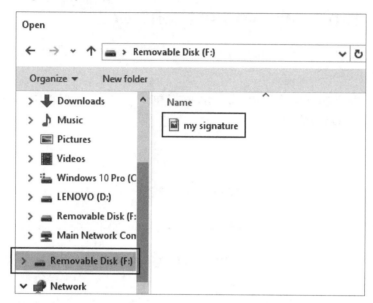

Remember that your USB flash drive may have a different name than what is shown here.

8. Click **Open**.

A thumbnail (small image) of the attachment is shown on the email.

9. Click **Send** and then close **Outlook.com**.

Receiving and Replying to Messages

Outlook.com checks for messages every thirty minutes and displays those messages in your Inbox. By default, messages are displayed from newest to oldest, but you can change that sort order if desired.

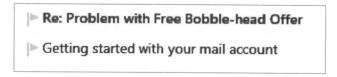

Messages that are unread will be in boldface type. Once you have opened a message, you have multiple options for handling it.

Replying

Replying enables you to quickly send a message back to the sender of an email. The Reply button enables you to reply to a message in three different ways.

TYPES OF REPLIES

Reply Type	What It Does
Reply	Replies only to the original sender of the email
Reply all	Replies to everyone who received the email
Forward	Enables you to forward a copy of the email to a new recipient, choosing to include or not include the original sender

HANDS-ON 5.5 Reply to an Email

In this exercise, you will reply to an email sent to you by your instructor.

Before You Begin: Have your instructor or someone else in your class send you an email. The content is not important.

1. Open **Outlook.com**.

2. Click on the email from your instructor.

3. Click the **Reply** button on the menu bar.
   Notice that a blank email appears with the instructor's address already in the address line and a copy of the previous message at the bottom of the email. Also notice that "RE:" has been added to the beginning of the subject line to indicate that you are replying to the original email.

4. Click **Cc** and type **sholten@lablearning.net**.

This will send a copy of the mail to Sarah Holten.

5. Type a short reply message and click **Send**.

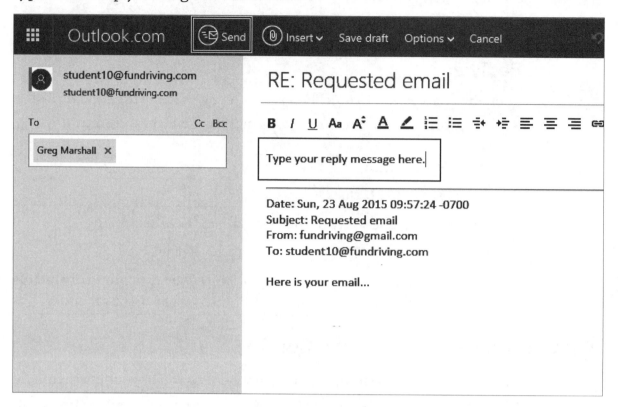

6. Close **Outlook.com**.

....

Deleting

If you don't need an email anymore, you can delete it. Deleted email is moved to the Deleted folder and is permanently removed after ten days. Once removed, you cannot get it back.

When viewing an email, if you want to delete it, you can use the Delete button on the menu bar.

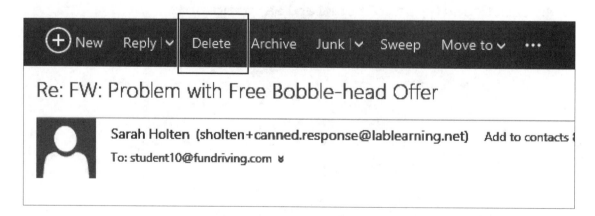

Saving Emails

The Inbox should not be used for saving emails. Doing this makes it difficult to see the new and recent emails you have to deal with as well as to find a specific email. Instead of storing emails in the Inbox, create folders.

Creating and Deleting Folders

Outlook.com enables you to create folders for sorting emails. Folders you create will appear on the Folders list on the left side of the screen along with the pre-made Outlook.com folders.

You can create folders for various activities like school, for a specific project, or even for specific timeframes like the quarters of the school year. The more organized your email is, the more efficient you will be at using it.

You can also delete folders that are no longer needed. When deleting a folder, you will get a warning message that any email in the folder will be deleted.

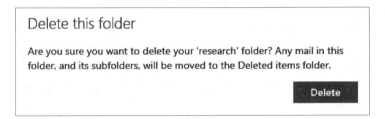

⚲ HANDS-ON 5.6 Create an Email Folder

In this exercise, you will create a folder for storing your important emails.

1. Start **Outlook.com**.

2. Click the **New Folder** command at the bottom of the Folders list.

A small text box appears above the command.

3. Type **Important Email** and tap ⌊Enter⌋.

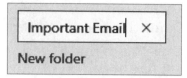

The folder Important Email appears above the New Folder command.

4. Create another folder called **Research**.

Delete a Folder

5. Right-click the **Research** folder and choose **Delete** from the menu.

6. Click **Delete** on the warning message that appears.
   Note that any messages in the folder will be permanently deleted along with the folder.

7. Close **Outlook.com**.

. . . .

Moving Emails

Outlook.com enables you to move emails to different folders in multiple ways. You can drag emails from the Inbox into the appropriate folder (the **drag-and-drop** method) or click in the checkbox to the left of the sender's name and use the Move To command. Each method accomplishes the same goal; use whichever method you prefer.

To move multiple files at one time, click the checkboxes for each email and then execute the move.

HANDS-ON 5.7 Move Emails

In this exercise, you will move emails to the Important Email folder using both the Move To method and the drag-and-drop method.

1. Open **Outlook.com**.

2. Click in the checkbox for the **Outlook.com Team** message to select it.

3. Click **Move To→Important Email**.

All the folders in the Folder list are listed on the Move To menu.

4. Click the **Important Email** folder in the Folder list and verify that your email is there.

Drag Emails to Folders

5. Click the **Inbox** folder.

6. Drag the email from **Douglas Campbell** over to the **Important Email** folder and release.

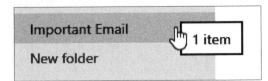

As you drag the file over to the Important Email folder, the mouse cursor will transform into a pointing hand holding a box. The number of items being moved is displayed on the envelope.

7. Click on the **Important Email** folder and verify that the file is there.

8. Close **Outlook.com**.

....

Saving Email Addresses

Outlook.com enables you to save email addresses so you don't have to retype them over and over again. These frequently used addresses appear under the address line.

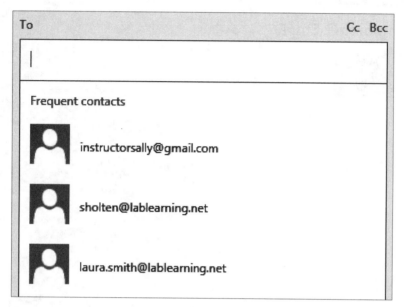

As you type an email address into the address line, the frequent contacts are filtered. When you see the address you want, you can click on it to add it to the address line.

Keep in touch. Some of the folks you just emailed aren't contacts yet. Do you want to add them? | Add contacts

Occasionally, Outlook.com will ask if you want to save a particular email address from an email that you have received. These messages will appear along the bottom of the Outlook.com window.

Email Safety

In a study done by IT security company Kaspersky Labs in the first quarter of 2013, they found that 70% of all email was unsolicited commercial email (spam) and that 2.4% of it had malicious attachments! Luckily, most problematic emails get filtered out before they reach your inbox.

Email represents one of the top ways your computer and devices are compromised, and the result can be machines that don't work, stolen information, compromised passwords, and wasted time.

With a few simple steps and a little bit of knowledge, you can dramatically reduce the threat malicious email poses to you.

Tip! Email is not secure. You should never send passwords, credit card numbers, personal information, or other sensitive information in an email message.

Understanding the Threats

What are the threats? There are four categories of malicious email activity: spam, phishing scams, advance fee scams, and spoofing.

Spam

Spam is as much a waste of time and resources as it is a threat. According to the US government, spam is unsolicited commercial email. Spam tries to sell products that may or may not be real in hopes of getting your credit card number and money. Once they have your credit card number, you may or may not get the product.

Phishing

Phishing (pronounced like fishing) scams are focused on getting credit card numbers, logins, passwords, and other personal information like Social Security numbers. Generally, the emails look like they are from a bank, the government, cable companies, or other big entities that you may do business with. The emails look "real," as they usually have company logos and addresses in them, but any Internet links they contain don't really go to the company. Remember...no government agency or business will *ever* ask you for your credit card number, login, password, or Social Security number via email. EVER.

The following is an example of a Bank of America phishing email. It looks real but is completely phony. You can tell it is phony, because Bank of America will never have you click links in an email; they will have you go to the bank site and login. They would also never have the most obvious link on the page be the one for declining a service. Finally, if you look closely at the message, you will see some spelling and grammatical errors, which a large company would not permit in important communications.

Exclusively for: | **Bank of America**

 Online Banking Alert
Email confirmation for Wire Transfers service

Checkpoint:
    You last logged in to Online Banking on 3/06/2013.
    Remember: Always look for your SiteKey® before entering your Passcode.

Welcome to the Transfers Outside Bank of America service, which lets you transfer between your Bank of America consumer deposit accounts and deposit accounts you own at other financial institutions.

For security purposes, please validate your   email address by signing in to Online Banking. (Remember: Always look for your Site Key before you sign in.) Then select the Transfer Funds, Make Transfer and Outside the Bank tabs, and follow the on-screen instructions.

You will need to submit the following code in order to Complete Money Transfer:

    (You also can copy and paste this code to avoid typing it in.)

Once validation is complete, you can begin adding the accounts you own at other financial institutions so that you can easily make transfers with those accounts.

Or open this link to Decline this operation if you did not issued the transaction or made it by mistake.

Thank you for using Online Banking.

_____

Security Checkpoint: This email includes a Post Control. The information in this section lets you know this is an authoritative informer from Bank of America. Remember to verify your SiteKey every time you logging in to Online Banking.

Email Preferences
This is a warning email from Bank of America. Please note that you may receive service message because of your Bank of America service agreements, whether or not you elect to

Spoofing

Spoofing is when someone forges an email address and sender name that makes the email look legitimate when it's not. Spoofing is often used as a part of other scams.

Advance Fee

Advance fee emails and scams try to get you to send money with the promise of great riches or deals. This scam plays on people's greed. In one form of this scam, a foreign person asks for your help because they have just inherited millions of dollars or have access to millions. They promise to share the money with you if you will advance them some funds to help move the inheritance to the United States.

```
RE: MR. RANDY CODY,
INVESTMENT MANAGER
PRIVATE & VERY SAFE
TONBRIDGE,
KENT TN11 9DZ,
UNITED KINGDOM .



I wish to inform you that this letter is not a hoax mail and I urge you to treat it serious. We want to transfer The
52,000,000.00 (Fifty Two Million
GBP) to any safe account with your honest assistance. I have every possibility for the accumulated proceed to be
paid in your favour and then both of us will share the value equal percentage Can I trust you on this?


Although, necessary steps has been made regards to this issue confidentially with key Bank Personnel?s and they have
agreed to help if I found honest and capable person to handle this transaction to enable us transfer the value Asset
out from UK.

I guarantee that this will be executed under a concrete special arrangement that will protect us from any breach of
law. I will not fail to bring to your notice that this transaction is total hitch-free and you should not entertain
any fear because good arrangement has been outlined for successful conclusion.

If you are willing and capable to handle this business with me in full confidence & trust, please do not hesitate to
Reply me back


I look forward hearing from you.

Warmest Regards.

MR. RANDY CODY,
```

An example of an advance fee scam email. If you were to respond to this email, eventually they would email you and ask for money.

Unfortunately, many people fall for these types of scams every year.

SPOTTING A MALICIOUS EMAIL

Sign	Why is it a sign?
Bad grammar and misspellings	No company will send an email that contains spelling errors. Many malicious emails comes from Africa, Russia, and Eastern Europe, where English is a second language.
It's too good to be true	This old saying applies to emails. If the deal is really good...it's probably an unsafe email.
Strange email from a friend	If you receive an email from a friend telling you to open the attachment or click on a link, or the message is not expected, only contains a link, and isn't personalized...it's probably an unsafe email.

Sign	Why is it a sign?
Personal email from someone you don't know	When someone's email or social media account is compromised, the email addresses of all their contacts are frequently spammed. For example, seniors may get emails from "grandkids" needing money to get out of a bind.
Unsolicited emails from the government or a private company	These emails may ask for your credit card numbers, login information, or Social Security number to "update your account," but government agencies and legitimate companies will always tell you to go directly to their site rather than requesting information in an email or having you follow a link.
The sender's email address has a domain that's a random series of characters	No legitimate company will have an email address that ends in something nonsensical, such as @2we34fgt.com.

Protecting Yourself

If you have read this far, you have done more to protect yourself than most people. Knowing what the threat looks like is half the battle.

Take the next steps to deal with spam and other malicious emails:

- Delete suspect emails—If you suspect that an email is spam or malicious, don't view it, click any links, or download any attachments. Doing so can trigger malicious actions attached to the email, such as installing a computer virus on your computer.

- Don't reply to spam—Replying to spam email lets the sender know that your email address is active and will increase the amount of spam you receive.

- Don't give out your email address—Limit who gets your email address. When signing up for free sites on the Internet, decide if it's really worth the spam you are going to get just to play a free game or activity.

Deleting Spam in Outlook.com

Besides automatically deleting known spam emails, Outlook.com gives you a way to remove spam that you receive.

 Using the Junk command on the menu bar moves the selected email to the Junk folder and marks the sender as unsafe. Email in the Junk folder is deleted after ten days.

HANDS-ON 5.8 Remove a Spam Message

In this exercise, you will remove a spam email using the Junk command.

1. Start **Outlook.com**.

2. Click the email from **Sarah Holten**.
   Notice that it has all the signs of a spam email—it's just way too good to be true.

3. Click the **Junk** command on the menu bar.
   You are now viewing the next email from your Inbox. Sarah's email has been moved to the Junk folder.

4. Click the **Junk** folder.
   Notice that Sarah's email is in there. It will automatically be deleted in ten days.

5. Click the **Inbox** folder.

6. Close **Outlook.com**.

. . . .

Concepts Review

To check your knowledge of the key concepts introduced in this chapter, complete the Concepts Review quiz on this page. Or, you can take the quiz online by going to **labyrinthelab/wtcb10**.

Page number

1. Email is made up of a local piece and a domain piece separated by an @ symbol.   **true false** _____

2. Outlook.com is the only free email app available on the Internet.   **true false** _____

3. You can only send an email to one recipient at a time.   **true false** _____

4. You can only attach documents to your emails.   **true false** _____

5. Outlook.com blocks much of the spam that is sent to you.   **true false** _____

6. Multiple emails can be moved to a folder at the same time.   **true false** _____

7. Which of the following IS NOT an Address line option?

   a. To

   b. Bcc

   c. Cc

   d. Tcc

   Page number: _____

8. Which of the following IS NOT an email threat?

   a. spoofing

   b. advance fee

   c. phishing

   d. sponging

   Page number: _____

9. The Move To command enables you to _____.

   a. move selected emails to folders in Outlook.com

   b. move selected emails to folders on your computer

   c. move selected emails to OneDrive

   d. All of the above

   Page number: _____

10. Which of the following is a potential sign of a malicious email?

    a. bad grammar and misspellings

    b. offer is too good to be true

    c. an email address with a domain containing random series of characters

    d. All of the above

    Page number: _____

Skill Builders

....

SKILL BUILDER 5.1 Save Files from Links

In this exercise, you will save some images to your USB drive that were sent to you as links. These files will be used in later chapters.

1. Open **Outlook.com**.

2. Click the message from **Sally Minh**.

3. If you receive a warning that some parts of the message have been blocked, click the **Show Content** link.

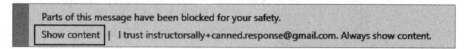

4. Click the link for **image1.png**.

   The image will be brought up in a new browser tab.

5. Right-click the image and choose **Save Picture** on the menu that appears.

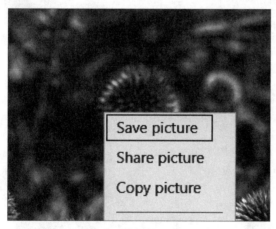

6. In the Save As dialog box, choose your USB flash drive as the save location and click **Save**. Keep the default name as image1.

7. Close the browser tab for **image1**.

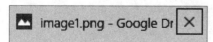

8. Repeat steps 4–7 for the remaining three images.

9. Close **Outlook.com**.

SKILL BUILDER 5.2 Create a Gmail Email Account

There are many free email clients available. In this exercise, you will create a free Gmail email account. The process used to create other email accounts is likely to have some similar steps.

1. Start **Edge**.

2. In the address bar type **mail.google.com** and click Enter.

3. Click the **Create an Account** button.

4. Enter the information requested in the form. Choose a Gmail email address and password. When asked for your existing email address, use the same one that you used when creating your Microsoft account.

Make sure to write down your new Gmail address and login.

5. Remove the checkmark next to **Set Google as My Default Homepage**.

6. Type the text that you see in the picture.

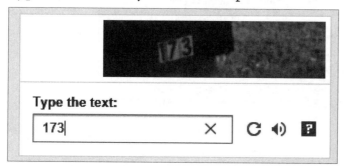

This is a captcha to prove you are not a robot making tons of fake email addresses. Your captcha will look different.

7. Put a checkmark next to "I agree to the Google Terms of Service..." and then click **Next Step**.

8. On the welcome screen, click **Continue to Gmail**.

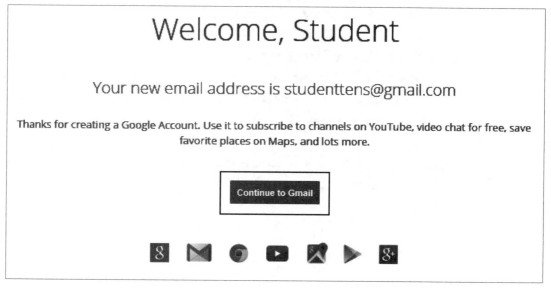

Your new Gmail login will enable you to log in to any Google site and app.

9. Close the **Gmail** pop-up that appears for new users.

10. Close the setup bar at the bottom of **Gmail**.

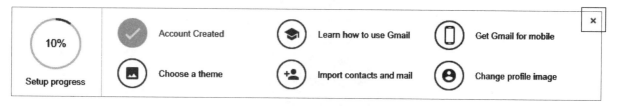

11. Close your browser.

SKILL BUILDER 5.3 Send and Read Email in Gmail

In this exercise, you will complete basic email procedures using Gmail.

1. Open **Edge** and go to **mail.google.com**.

2. Click the red **Compose** button on the left side of the screen.

This brings up a New Message dialog box, similar to the one seen in Outlook.com.

3. Type the following message:

To: laura.smith@lablearning.net

Subject: Crushed Bobble-Head

To Whom It May Concern, Enter
Enter
I just received my bobble-head doll, and it was crushed. The shipping package was in good shape, so it looks like it was damaged at the warehouse and shipped to me. Enter
Enter
I would like to know if a new bobble-head doll could be shipped to me. Enter
Enter
Thank you, Enter
Your Name

4. Click **Send** on the bottom-left corner of the email.
    Your message is sent and a confirmation appears at the top of the screen.

Your message has been sent. **View message**

5. When the email appears, click on the subject line of the email **Crushed Bobble-Head**.

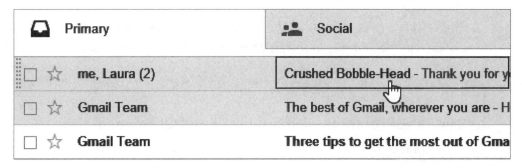

Notice the full email appears in Gmail with an area for you to Reply or Forward the email.

6. Click the right arrow button on the top-right of Gmail to read the next email.

Notice that Gmail shows the next email and that the newer button is now active. The back button allows you to go back to the previous email.

7. Click the **Back to Inbox** button.

SKILL BUILDER 5.4 Delete and Archive Emails in Gmail

In this exercise, you will delete and archive emails in your Gmail account. To archive a message means to store it in a different folder. The message will not clutter your Inbox, but it's also not deleted, so if you need it again later, you can easily retrieve it.

1. Click the checkbox next to one of the emails from the Gmail Team.

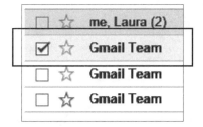

This selects the email. Multiple emails can be selected by clicking the checkboxes next to them.

2. Click the **Delete** button on the Gmail menu bar.

The selected email is sent to the Trash, and a confirmation appears at the top of the Gmail window. Emails in the trash are permanently deleted after thirty days.

The conversation has been moved to the Trash and will be permanently deleted in 30 days. Learn more Undo

3. Select the **Problems with Bobble-Head Offer** email.

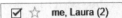
me, Laura (2)   Problems with Bobble-Head Offer - Thank you for your message. Due to high demand, we

4. Click the **Archive** button.

The email is archived and can be accessed later if needed.

The conversation has been archived. Learn more Undo

5. Close **Edge**.

....

SKILL BUILDER 5.5 Forward an Email

In this exercise, you will forward an email to a new recipient.

1. Open **Outlook.com**.

2. Click the email from **Douglas Campbell** located in the Important email folder.

3. Click the **Reply** drop-down arrow and choose **Forward**.

4. Type `sholten@lablearning.net` in the Send line.
   Notice that the Subject line already has been filled out and starts with "FW:," which notifies the recipient that the email is a copy being forwarded.

5. In the message area type: `It is great to see a company take responsibility for a mistake. I hope they can find me a bobble-head doll.`
   Notice that a copy of the original message has already been added.

6. Click **Send**.

7. Close **Outlook.com**.

....

UNIT 2: FILE MANAGEMENT

In this unit, you will explore ways to manage and organize files using Windows 10. Topics covered in Chapter 6 include the different types of storage media available for your use as well as how to use File Explorer to navigate and search for folders and files. In Chapter 7, you will explore how to create, move, copy, delete, and restore folders and files, and you will also learn about and use Microsoft's OneDrive file storage.

Finding Files

CHAPTER OBJECTIVES

- Describe and use various storage devices
- Use File Explorer to locate files and folders
- Plug in and properly unplug a USB flash drive
- Identify different types of folders used by Windows
- Find files and folders with File Search

Finding your files when you need them is obviously important. In this chapter, you will learn where to find a file you have created. You also will also learn how files, folders, and drives are organized on your computer so you can navigate through the system. Finally, you will become familiar with the search tools in Windows that can help you find files that have been misplaced.

Learning Resources: **labyrinthelab.com/wtcb10**

📁 Case Study: Checking Up on the Hard Drive

Jamal has had his computer for a while, and he is growing concerned about two potential problems:

- Since he has a digital camera, he thinks the pictures he has been saving on his computer may fill the hard drive to its maximum capacity.

- He also worries that all of his files would be lost if he were to have a fire in his house or if the hard drive in his computer were to fail.

A friend suggests that Jamal could save backup copies of the files on one or more external hard drives. Because an external hard drive is portable, he could keep it in his desk at work. The external hard drive at work would keep the backup copies of his files safe from disasters at home.

Jamal first decides to determine the capacity of his hard drive and how much of it is being used. His friend shows him how to determine the capacity of the hard drive by looking at its Properties box. It looks like this:

Jamal sees that the drive is not very full, so he decides to buy an external hard drive with a capacity of at least 500 GB and start backing up his files on the new drive on a regular basis.

About Storage Media

On most computers, you have many options for saving files you have created. Some of these storage devices are internal (inside the computer) and can't be moved. Others are portable and can be moved from computer to computer.

Types of Storage Devices

All of these devices can be used to store the various types of files you create, including documents, pictures, music, and videos.

Internal Hard Drive

This is the *permanent* storage inside the computer. Most of your files and all of the apps that run on your computer reside on this internal drive.

CD/DVD Drives

You can save files and folders on CDs or DVDs, and these are just like the ones your music and movies are saved on when you purchase them from a store. CDs and DVDs are used to store files because of their large storage capacity and their portability.

External Hard Drives

You can purchase hard drives that plug into your computer through a USB port (drives are discussed in the Behind the Screen: Drive Designations section on page 158). These external drives work just like internal hard drives, with the added advantage of being portable, enabling you to access your files from multiple computers.

USB Flash Drives

USB flash drives are sometimes referred to as keychain drives or thumb drives, and they are a type of removable storage. These small, key-sized drives allow you to easily carry files between computers at home, work, or anywhere.

You may have already used a USB flash drive to save your files in earlier chapters of this book. This chapter will provide you with more tips on using your USB flash drive.

Network Drives

Sometimes your computer will be connected to hard drives on other computers via a network. Although network drives may be located in another room or building, these remote drives can be used just like an internal drive or a portable storage device plugged into a USB port.

Viewing Storage Drives

In an office, you might store your paper files in a filing cabinet. The filing cabinet could have one drawer or many drawers. Storage on your computer is similar. Each storage device is like a drawer in a filing cabinet. Most desktop computers have two or more drives included: an internal hard drive and possibly a CD/DVD burner. Many laptops running Windows 10 do not have a CD/DVD burner. If you attach a USB flash drive to your computer, it is like having another drawer in which you can store data. Computers attached to a network may have access to even more drives.

Drive Letters

Windows provides an orderly process for dealing with multiple drives. Each drive is assigned a **drive letter** to help identify it. Obviously, you need to be able to view the drives and their drive letters, as well as the data stored on the drives, for them to be useful. File Explorer is the Windows feature that lets you view the drives and their data. (File Explorer is covered in more detail later in this chapter.)

Viewing the Drives

The Computer window lets you view the drives and then open the drives to see the data stored on them. In the following illustration, notice that File Explorer has grouped together the hard disk drives and the devices with removable storage. It also has displayed the drive names, drive letters, and information about each drive's capacity.

Some new computers will have two internal hard drive designations (C: and D:). The D: drive usually contains a backup of the computer's original software in case Windows needs to be reinstalled.

Some Windows 10 computers will have a DVD/CD drive. It uses removable discs for storage.

This is a USB flash drive that has been identified as a removable storage device and assigned the letter F:.

Many computers, laptops, and devices now come with SD card drives like those found on cameras.

Drive Designations

History

Storage devices or drives in the computer are designated with letters of the alphabet followed by a colon (:). The alphabet letter and colon combination has been around since the early beginnings of computers, when there were no graphic images to represent drives.

What Determines Drive Order?

Numerous drives can be connected to your computer, and there are logical reasons why drives are assigned certain letters—at least for the first few drives in your computer.

Drive designations A: and B: are reserved for **floppy disk** drives. For years, this was the most common portable storage device. Computers sold now do not come with floppy drives; USB flash drives and SD card readers have replaced them.

The C: drive is always the main internal drive in the computer. This is the drive on which the Windows software resides.

After the first three drive designations, the rules change a bit. You will see drives in various combinations and orders depending on how the computer is configured. Internal drives get designated first, starting with hard drives, followed by CDs and DVDs. Network drives are assigned next. External drives are last and are generally assigned designations based on the order in which they are attached to the computer.

An example of a computer with six drives connected and four network drive connections. The red bar means that drive is really full!

Tip! Two important things to remember about drive letter assignments: 1) The main internal drive in the computer will always be drive C: and 2) your USB flash drive *will not necessarily have the same letter designation* on every computer with which it is used.

HANDS-ON 6.1 View Drives on Your Computer

In this exercise, you will view the various drives on your computer.

1. Choose **Start** ⊞→**File Explorer**.

The File Explorer window appears.

2. Click **This PC** on the left side of the screen. Look at all the devices and drives listed on the right side of the screen.

3. **Close** ⊠ the **File Explorer** window.

Plugging In and Unplugging a Flash Drive

There is more to using a USB flash drive than simply inserting and removing it from a USB port on your computer. Your USB flash drive must be recognized by Windows when it is first plugged in and safely unplugged to avoid damage to data stored on the drive.

Plugging In

Your USB flash drive can be plugged into any USB port on a computer, but before you can use it, Windows must recognize the drive. Recognition can take a few moments.

Unplugging Safely

Before you remove your USB flash drive, you must make sure Windows is no longer using the drive for any reason, such as saving a file. There is a risk of damaging the files on the USB flash drive if it is unplugged improperly. There are two primary methods to unplug a USB flash drive while the computer is running (you can always safely unplug the drive after you properly shut down the computer):

- **Activity light method:** If a USB flash drive has a blinking activity light, do not unplug the drive until a few seconds after the light stops blinking.

- **Safely Remove Hardware and Eject Media command:** If you want to be absolutely sure the drive can be unplugged safely, use the Safely Remove Hardware and Eject Media command. Windows will then notify you when all activity on the USB flash drive stops so you can unplug it.

QUICK REFERENCE: Safely Unplugging a USB Flash Drive

Task	Procedure
Use the Safely Remove Hardware and Eject Media command	- Close ⊠ all windows being used by the USB flash drive. - If necessary, click the Show Hidden Icons ⌃ button on the notification area so all icons are visible. - Click the Safely Remove Hardware and Eject Media 🖥 icon. - Choose the drive you wish to unplug from the list. - Once the dialog box appears that tells you the device can safely be removed, unplug the drive.
Safely unplug using the activity light	- Close ⊠ all windows being used by the USB flash drive. Wait a few seconds after the activity light stops blinking, and then unplug the device.

HANDS-ON 6.2 View Your USB Flash Drive

In this exercise, you will properly plug in your USB flash drive to the computer, open and close a file, and then safely unplug the flash drive.

1. Choose **Start** ⊞→**File Explorer**.

2. Insert your USB flash drive into an available USB port on the computer and click **This PC** in the navigation pane of File Explorer.

   Once your drive is recognized, it will show up in the File Explorer window under the Devices and Drives section, as shown in the following illustration. At this point, the USB flash drive is recognized and can be used like any other storage device on the computer. Take note of the name and drive letter, because you will use these later in the exercise.

   ✓ Devices and drives (4)

   Windows 10 Pro (C:)
   367 GB free of 425 GB

   LENOVO (D:)
   22.1 GB free of 24.9 GB

   DVD RW Drive (E:)

   Removable Disk (F:)
   7.48 GB free of 7.52 GB

3. **Close** ⨉ the AutoPlay window if it appears.

4. Double-click to open your USB flash drive.

   Windows displays the contents of the drive. If you used this drive in Chapter 4, Working with Apps, you should see the documents and Paint pictures you created in that lesson.

5. Once the light on the USB flash drive has stopped blinking, you can safely unplug the drive from the computer.

   If your USB flash drive does not have a blinking light, use the steps mentioned earlier in the chapter to safely remove your hardware.

File Explorer

File Explorer (or simply Explorer) lets you view a computer's drives and the data on them. The following figure displays some of the key features of an Explorer window.

The address bar shows where you are in the drive and folder system. It also lets you move around in the drive and folder system.

The Search box allows you to look for files and folders.

The Folders pane lets you view all folders on all drives.

The View pane shows you everything in the selected drive or folder. Here, since This PC is selected, we're seeing all drives.

Note! Throughout the rest of this book, the File Explorer window will be referred to as a folder window.

Common Folder Window Tasks

The folder window allows you to perform a number of useful tasks:

- **browsing** for files and folders

- **searching** for files and folders

- **creating** new folders and using them to organize your documents

- **renaming** files and folders

- **moving and copying** files and folders

- **deleting** files and folders

This chapter concentrates on the first two tasks—browsing and searching. The other tasks will be covered in Chapter 7, Storing Files.

Note! Don't confuse File Explorer with Internet Explorer. File Explorer is used to explore drives, folders, and files on your computer; Internet Explorer is a web browser used to explore the Internet.

Locating Folders

When a new login name is created, Windows creates a set of folders on the internal hard drive. These folders are intended to be the storage locations for that individual's folders and files. Because of their importance as a person's primary storage locations, Windows also provides quick access commands to these folders from various locations, such as the Start menu and folder windows.

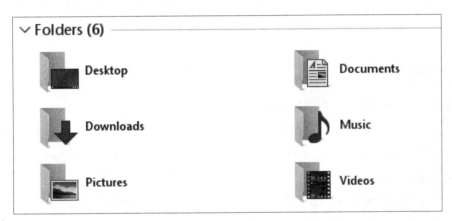

Tip! You can distinguish these folders from normal folders because they have custom graphics.

Navigating Your Drives and Folders

Being able to navigate drives and folders to locate your files is a critical skill. There are three easy-to-use navigation features built into the folder window:

- Address bar

- Folders pane

- Back and Forward buttons

Folders and Subfolders

Files are organized using folders. Folders can be further organized by adding more folders within them called **subfolders**. Any folder can have subfolders. This system is like having a filing cabinet drawer full of files organized into folders.

The Photos folder has a subfolder called February. The February folder also has a subfolder called Best.

The Address Bar

The address bar runs across the top of a folder window and displays a **path** (hierarchy) that includes a starting location and any drive, folders, or subfolders linked to the location that are currently open. The path is like a map with signs pointing to your present location, and it is File Explorer's way of saying, "You are here, and this is how you got here." You can see how to navigate to your present location by following the path toward the left.

This path begins with the Computer folder on the left.

The folder currently being viewed (February) is at the right end of the path.

As you move left through the path toward its beginning, you are navigating up the folder structure.

Navigating via the Address Bar

The subfolders listed in the path actually are buttons that, when clicked, open that subfolder in the folder window. Each subfolder in the path also has a drop-down menu that shows its subfolders (accessed with the menu button). The subfolders on the drop-down menu also display in the folder window if clicked. You can navigate (browse) the folder structure of the path using these subfolder buttons and drop-down menus.

The menu button displays a list of subfolders in the Photos folder.

QUICK REFERENCE: Navigating with the Address Bar Path

Task	Procedure
Move to a different folder on the path	■ Move your mouse pointer over a folder name on the path to see its button and then click. `Photos ›`
Move to a subfolder in a folder on the path	■ Move your mouse pointer over the menu button to see its button and then click. `›` ■ Click a subfolder on the drop-down list. `January`

HANDS-ON 6.3 Navigate Using the Address Bar

In this exercise, you will use the address bar to navigate within your personal folders.

1. Choose **Start** ⊞ →**File Explorer**.

2. Follow these steps to navigate to the Pictures folder:

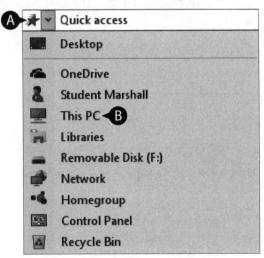

Ⓐ Click the menu › button on the address bar to the right of the Quick Access star.

Ⓑ Choose the **This PC** folder from the list.

Windows displays the content of This PC, which includes the Picture folder.

3. Click the menu › button to the right of This PC on the address bar and choose **Pictures**.

The View pane displays the content of the Pictures folder, and the folder's name is added to the path on the address bar.

4. Close **File Explorer**.

. . . .

The Back and Forward Buttons

The Back and Forward buttons remember the order of the folders that you have viewed. If you choose to view a subfolder and then change your mind, the Back button will change your view back to your previous folder.

If you change your mind again, you can return to the subfolder you were just viewing by using the Forward button. The buttons work a lot like the back and forward buttons on a DVD player's remote control that allow you to move back and forth through the frames of a movie.

- The Back button takes you back to previously viewed locations in the reverse order of the way they were originally viewed.

- The Forward button doesn't work until you move back at least one step. (This is why that button is usually grayed out.)

Tip! The Back and Forward buttons in Microsoft Edge work just like the buttons in a folder window.

HANDS-ON 6.4 Use the Back and Forward Buttons

In this exercise, you will use the Back and Forward buttons in a folder window to navigate folders.

1. Choose **Start** ⊞→**File Explorer**.

2. Choose **This PC**.

3. Double-click the **Pictures** folder.

    The View pane (right panel) now displays the contents of the Pictures folder. Notice that the Forward button is faded, which indicates the button is inactive. The Forward button won't work until you use the Back button at least once.

4. Click the **Back** button to move back into This PC.

    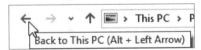

    Windows returns you to the previous view—in this case, This PC. Notice that the Forward button is now colored, indicating that it is active.

5. Click the **Forward** button to return to the Pictures folder.

    Windows moves you forward to the folder from which you had moved back, which in this case is to the Pictures folder.

6. Close **File Explorer**.

Units of Measure for Computer Storage

Size and capacity in the computer world are based on the byte, which is the smallest unit of measurement in the computer world. When you are typing a letter, each character you type is one byte of information.

Measurement	Abbreviations	Is Equal to...
Byte		1 character (e.g., a, b, !, etc.)
Kilobyte	KB or "K"	1,024 bytes
Megabyte	MB or "meg"	1,024 kilobytes
Gigabyte	GB or "gig"	1,024 megabytes
Terabyte	TB	1,024 gigabytes

Note! This note is especially for math junkies! Notice that all the numbers end in 24. This is because computer numbers tend to be based on factors of 8. To simplify these numbers, they are often rounded to the nearest thousand.

Common Data File Sizes

Different types of data that you create will require different amounts of storage space. A basic rule of thumb is that the more complicated the file, the more space it needs. A photo will need more space than a typed document; a home video will need more space than a photo.

Item	Approximate Size
Word-processing document	20–30 K per page
Digital camera photo	1–7 MB, depending on your camera, the picture's quality, and its size
Music file	3–6 MB per song, depending on the audio quality and song length
Video file	1–20 MB for every 30 seconds, depending on the video's quality and format
HD video	1.7 MB per second or 50–55 MB per 30 seconds

The View Tab

The way folder and file information is displayed in File Explorer can be changed using commands in the View tab. Other commands in the View tab change how the information shown in the View pane is sorted.

Layout

The Layout commands change how files and folders are presented in the folder pane. The various commands not only change the size of the file icons but also the amount of information shown for each file, folder, or drive.

As you work with files and folders, you may find that some views work better than others for various tasks.

Tip! Folder and drive windows remember their view settings when closed. You may want to change the view as you complete the exercises to more closely match the exercise figures.

Sorting

By default, most folders are sorted with subfolders showing first, followed by files. Everything is sorted alphabetically by name from A to Z. This arrangement can be changed using the Sort By button.

With the Sort By drop-down menu, you can choose from other key pieces of information to sort by and change from ascending to descending sort order. This can be very useful when looking for a specific file. For example, when you can't find a file you were just looking for, you can sort by Date Modified, and files will be sorted with the ones most recently changed at the top of the window.

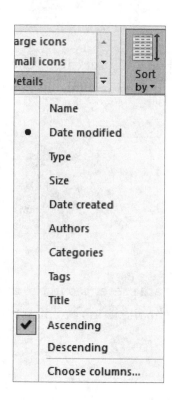

COMMON SORT FILTERS

Filter	Explanation
Name	The default sort order for files in all folders
Date Modified	Sorts files by the last time they were changed (saved)
Type	Sorts files by type (e.g., all Paint files followed by all text files)
Size	Sorts files by their size
Ascending	Modifies the chosen sort; A–Z, smallest to biggest, etc. (Ascending is the default setting).
Descending	Modifies the chosen sort; Z-A, biggest to smallest, etc.

Tip! In some locations in File Explorer, when you work with drives or network locations, the list of filters on the Sort By button may be different.

HANDS-ON 6.5 Sort Folders

In this exercise, you will sort the folders on the local disk (C: drive).

1. Choose **Start**→**File Explorer**.

2. Click **This PC**.

3. Under the Devices and Drives section, double-click **Local Disk (C:)**. Your drive C: may have a different name.

File Explorer shows all the folders that contain Windows as well as the apps on your computer. By default they are in alphabetical order (unless someone else has changed the sort already).

4. Click **Sort By** and then choose **Date Modified**.
   Notice the folders are now ordered by the date they were last changed.

5. Click the **View** tab, then choose **Sort By**→**Name**.

6. Change the sort order from Ascending to **Descending**.
   Notice that the folders are now organized from Z–A.

7. Close **File Explorer**.

Identifying the Contents of a Folder

The icons used to identify folders can tell you a lot about the kind of information stored in that folder. Windows changes the look of a folder icon (in certain views) to help you identify whether it holds subfolders or files, as well as to indicate the file types. The folders will look different on each computer and may change over time, depending on the files available in the folder for making the representations. The following table shows some of the common folder icons seen in Windows 10.

Folder Type	Description	Folder Type	Description
Basic Folder	This folder may be empty.	Graphics	This folder contains only graphics and displays actual pictures.
Multiple Files and Folders	When multiple file types are in the same folder, a generic folder like this is used.	Documents	This folder contains documents. It may display program icons from Microsoft Office and other software.
Music	This folder contains music; it displays album covers, if available.	Videos	This folder contains videos. It displays the first frame of a video or program icon.

The Folders Pane

The Folders pane enables you to select files from a more complete view of the folder "tree" (hierarchy), starting with This PC. The Folders pane displays all the drives and folders on your computer, plus any attached external drives and their folders. When you click a folder, the contents of that folder are displayed in the View pane to the right of the Folders pane.

The Folders pane is showing the hierarchy structure of all the drives and folders.

The contents of the selected drive or folder in the Folders pane are shown in the View pane to the right.

Expanding Subfolders

Some folders may have an expand view ▸ button on the left. The expand view button enables you to see the subfolders in that folder. When clicked, the folder expands to show its subfolders without changing the View pane. When the arrow button is pointing down, it indicates that the folder is expanded.

The expand view button shows that the folder has subfolders to view.

When the button is pointing down, the folder is expanded and you can see all the subfolders.

⌾ HANDS-ON 6.6 Navigate Using the Folders Pane

In this exercise, you will use the Folders pane to navigate among folders.

1. Choose **Start→File Explorer**.

2. **Maximize** ⬜ the folder window.

3. Follow these steps to navigate using the Folders pane:

Ⓐ Click the expand view button next to This PC (if necessary) to expand the folder.

Ⓑ Click to expand **Pictures**.

Ⓒ Choose the **Saved Pictures** folder from the list.

The View pane now shows the contents of the Saved Pictures folder. Depending on what others have done on the computer, there may or may not be many (or even any) items in this folder.

4. **Close** ⨯ the window.

Searching for Files

Windows' Search feature allows you to easily look for lost files or folders. By typing in part of a filename or some text from a file, Search displays (filters) the files and folders it finds that match your search text. Search can help you locate any type of file including music, graphics, and text files.

By default, Search automatically looks at files in the folder you are currently viewing, plus all of your personal folders, including Documents, Pictures, Music, and many more.

Windows gathers information about your various documents in the background while you work. This information is collected in a large index that makes Search work faster and more accurately.

When you start typing search words into the Search box, Windows displays all related files and folders.

The green bar shows the progress of your search.

Note! Search may not seem important now, but as your music library grows or you start using a digital camera, the number of files in your personal folders may blossom into the thousands. Without Search, finding lost files could become tedious.

⏚ HANDS-ON 6.7 Find a File with Windows Search

In this exercise, you will use Search to locate all text files on This PC.

1. Choose **Start** ⊞ →**File Explorer**.

2. Click **This PC**.

3. Type **txt** in the Search box.

Notice that as you start typing text, Windows immediately starts looking for files and folders that match your search.

4. Click the **Close** ⨯ button at the end of the Search box to return to displaying all files in This PC.

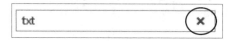

5. Close **File Explorer**.

· ·

Concepts Review

To check your knowledge of the key concepts introduced in this chapter, complete the Concepts Review quiz on this page. Or, you can take the quiz online by going to **labyrinthelab/wtcb10**.

Page number

1. You can securely remove a USB flash drive by unplugging it at any time.   **true false** _____

2. You can use Search to find music and pictures as well as documents.   **true false** _____

3. Every login name has its own personal folders.   **true false** _____

4. USB flash drives are often called thumb drives.   **true false** _____

5. Folders can contain other folders (subfolders).   **true false** _____

6. By default, Search will look for files only in the folder you are currently viewing.   **true false** _____

7. You can navigate to drives and folders using all of the following except the _____.

   a. address bar

   b. Folders pane

   c. Search pane

   d. Back and Forward buttons

   Page number: _____

8. In a folder window, you can navigate to various folders using the _____.

   a. address bar

   b. Back and Forward buttons

   c. Folders pane

   d. All of the above

   Page number: _____

9. How do you securely unplug a USB flash drive?

   a. Use the Safely Remove Hardware and Eject Media icon in the notification area.

   b. Close all open programs and gently remove it from the USB port once the activity light stops blinking.

   c. Shut down the computer properly and remove the drive from the USB port.

   d. All of the above

   Page number: _____

10. A USB flash drive is a(n) _____.

    a. removable storage device

    b. internal storage device

    c. temporary storage device

    d. network storage device

    Page number: _____

Skill Builders

Find the Remaining Capacity of a Drive

In this exercise, you will explore your USB flash drive. First you'll discover which folders and files are stored on the drive.

1. Choose **Start** ⊞→**File Explorer**.

2. Plug your USB flash drive into a USB port on the computer.
   Depending on how it is configured, Windows 10 probably will open an AutoPlay window asking what you want to do with the newly plugged-in drive.

3. Click **This PC**.

4. Open any folders on your USB flash drive to see what data has been stored, or continue with the next step if there aren't any folders on the drive.

5. Double-click on the icon for your **USB flash drive**.
   Are there any subfolders? What file types (data, photos, music) have you copied to the drive?

Find Out How Much Free Space Is Available

Now you will give a command to display the available space on your USB flash drive.

6. Click **This PC**.

7. Right-click the **USB flash drive** icon and choose **Properties**.

Windows displays a pie chart and details about the storage space on your flash drive.

The Properties dialog box shows how much space is used and how much is available.

8. Click **OK**.

9. Close **File Explorer**.

SKILL BUILDER 6.2 **Search the Contents of Files**

In this exercise, you will find files by looking for content within the file itself.

1. Choose **Start** ▦ →**File Explorer**.

2. Click **This PC**.

3. Click in the **Search** box.

4. Click the **Search** tab.

5. Click the **Advanced Options** command and choose **File Contents** from the drop-down menu.

The file search will now look for search terms within document-type files.

6. Click in the **Search** box and type `internet`.

   Depending on the number of files on your computer, the search may take some time. Notice that the files being shown don't necessarily have the word internet in their filename.

7. Click the **Close** ☒ button on the Search box.

8. Choose **Search Tools**→**Search**→**Advanced Options**→**File Contents** to deselect it.

   We don't want to leave this option on, as it will slow down future searches.

9. Close **File Explorer**.

CHAPTER 7

Storing Files

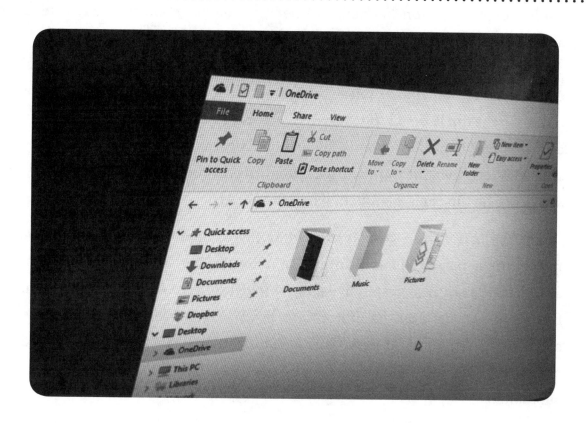

LEARNING OBJECTIVES

- Create new folders and subfolders for organizing your files

- Move or copy folders and files from one location to another

- Delete folders and files and, if necessary, restore them from the Recycle Bin

- Use OneDrive to store your files and folders

- Upload to and download from OneDrive

At some point after you have saved drawings from Paint and letters from Word Online or transferred pictures from your digital camera, you will want to organize these digital files. Windows provides methods for organizing files that are similar to how you would organize a filing cabinet in an office. In this chapter, you will create folders, move files around between folders, and work with the Recycle Bin to retrieve accidently deleted files. You will also spend time organizing files on OneDrive, your cloud storage location.

Learning Resources: labyrinthelab.com/wtcb10

📁 Case Study: Getting Organized

Aileen has been creating and saving many different file types on her computer. She has lots of pictures from her digital camera, a large collection of her favorite songs, all kinds of homework from a half dozen classes—and a big mess. Her photos are stuffed into the Pictures folder like pictures thrown in a shoebox. Her music collection is reasonably organized, but she would like to put some of the songs online so she can listen to them at work. The biggest mess is her homework. It has all been saved in her Documents folder, but assignments from different classes are all mixed together. She wants all the homework from each class to be grouped, so she can easily find an assignment when she needs it.

Aileen has learned how to make subfolders. She decides to organize her personal folders the same way she would organize a filing cabinet. In Documents, she creates a subfolder for each semester, makes a subfolder for each class within the semester folders, and then moves the appropriate files into each folder. For her pictures, she creates folders for different years and months in the Pictures folder. She also creates copies of pictures she used for homework and puts the copies into the class subfolders.

Aileen is pleased with her first attempt at organizing her files.

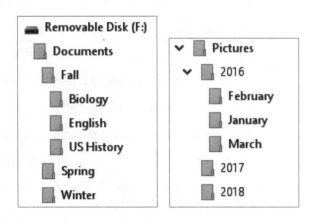

Creating Folders

The purpose of having folders in the Windows system is to make it easier to organize the thousands of files on your computer. Electronic folders enable you to organize files into groups, such as a folder for your Maui pictures or one for your science projects. Although each person will have their own organizational style, certain conventions must be followed as you create new folders:

- Folders can be created in another folder, on a drive, on OneDrive, or on the Desktop.

- The naming conventions for folders are the same as those for naming files. Refer to the Naming Files table in Chapter 4. A folder name (including its entire path) can be up to 255 characters long and include some symbols, such as dashes, commas, ampersands, and apostrophes.

- You cannot have two folders with identical names in the same location. Windows will merge the two folders.

Creating New Folders

There are two commonly used procedures for creating new folders: using the New Folder button in the folder window and choosing from the pop-up menu (also called a right-click menu).

QUICK REFERENCE: Creating Folders

Task	Procedure
Create a new folder via the New Folder button	<ul><li>Open the folder or drive where you want to put a new folder.</li><li>Choose Home→New Folder from the Ribbon.</li><li>Type the new folder name and tap Enter.</li></ul>
Create a new folder via the right-click method	<ul><li>Navigate to the location (Desktop, folder, or drive) where you want to put a new folder.</li><li>Right-click a blank place in the window or on the Desktop and choose New→Folder.</li><li>Type the new folder name and tap Enter.</li></ul>

Note! The Desktop is a folder that can be viewed in a folder window, which is where the New Folder command will be available. However, usually you see the Desktop as your opening screen without menus, so in this case, use the right-click method to create a new folder.

How Files Are Stored in Your Computer

There is an order to how your computer stores files on its various internal and external drives. The process for storing files is similar to procedures you might use to organize a filing cabinet—individual files might be grouped by subject, put inside folders, and labeled with an appropriate name. If there are many files within a folder, you might create subfolders to subdivide the primary folder into more specific groups. The drives on a computer are organized in a similar manner, using electronic folders, subfolders, and files.

Folders and Subfolders Created by Windows

Program Files   Program Files (x86)   Users   Windows

System folders installed on your local C: drive by Windows

Electronic folders, subfolders, and files are created when Windows is installed on the local hard drive (C:) of your computer. Windows is a very large collection of programs with thousands of system files that are stored on your internal hard drive. The purpose of the system files is to help the computer carry out all of the tasks necessary to run Windows.

Most of Windows' system files are stored in a folder named Windows. The files in the folder are grouped into several thousand subfolders. When a new application program is installed onto your hard drive, some of the program files may be stored in the Windows folder, but the rest of the files are grouped into a folder with a name chosen by the manufacturer. This folder is then stored in the folder named Program Files.

As new users are added to your computer, a subfolder for each—named after the user—is created inside Windows' Users folder. Windows also creates 11 personal subfolders for each user to help them organize their documents, pictures, music, videos, and other common types of files.

System folders installed on local drive C:

Program Files   Program Files (x86)   Users   Windows

AMD
AMD Quick Stream
ATI
ATI Technologies
Common Files
CONEXANT
Dolby Digital Plus

Default.migrated
Greg
Public
stude
Student
Video
websi

addins
ADFS
appcompat
AppPatch
AppReadiness
assembly
Boot
Branding

Subfolders created by Windows and nested inside the C: drive folders

Thousands of folders and subfolders are created by Windows on your local hard drive.

Renaming Files and Folders

Sometimes you will want to correct or change the name of a file or folder. You must follow Windows' naming conventions, mentioned previously, when you do so. You also can select and rename multiple files or folders simultaneously. When you rename a folder with the name of an existing folder in the same location, Windows will ask if you want to merge the two folders.

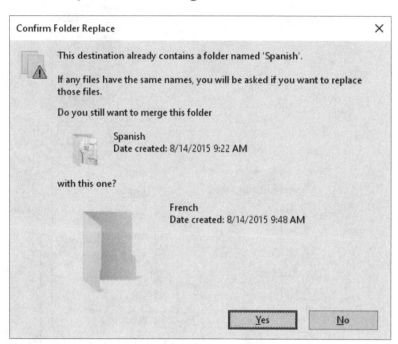

QUICK REFERENCE: Renaming Files or Folders

Task	Procedure
Rename files or folders from a toolbar menu	▪ Open the file/folder location and select the item(s) to be renamed. ▪ Choose Home→Organize→Rename. ▪ Type the new name and tap Enter.
Rename files or folders using a right-click	▪ Open the file/folder location and select the item(s) to be renamed. ▪ Right-click a selected item and choose Rename. ▪ Type the new name and tap Enter.

⌘ HANDS-ON 7.1 Create a New Folder on the Desktop

In this exercise, you will create and name a new folder on the Desktop. Then you will rename it.

Since there are no menus displayed on the Desktop for creating a folder, use the right-click method to display a pop-up menu that will allow you to create one.

1. Follow these steps to create a new folder on the Desktop:

   Ⓐ Right-click on a clear area of the Desktop to display its pop-up menu.

   Ⓑ Choose **New**.

   Ⓒ Click **Folder**.

   The new folder appears with its name selected, ready for you to type a new one.

2. To name the folder, type **Practice** and tap ⌐Enter⌐.

3. Create another folder called **More Practice** and tap ⌐Enter⌐.

Rename the Folder

4. Right-click the **Practice** folder and choose **Rename**.

5. Type the new name **Delete Practice** and tap ⌐Enter⌐.

6. Right-click the **More Practice** folder and rename it **Junk Folder**.

Creating Subfolders

When a folder gets filled with files, you may wish to divide the files into groups using subfolders. Those subfolders can have their own subfolders, and so on. Subfolders are also called *nested* folders. When a new login name, such as Student, is created, Windows creates a User folder named Student along with a bunch of subfolders (including Documents, Pictures, and Music) that are nested inside. If you then nest two subfolders named Animals and Flowers inside the Pictures folder, the *path* (hierarchy) looks like this.

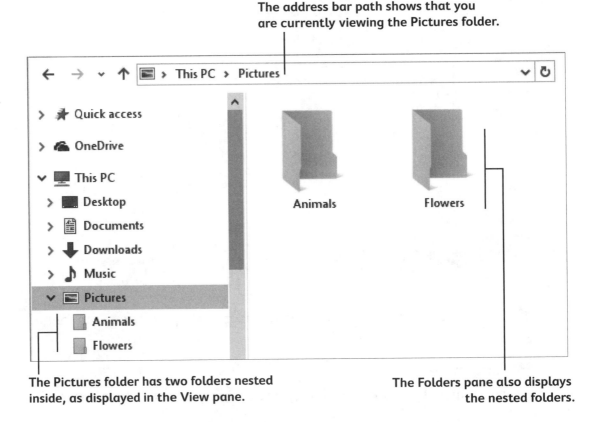

The address bar path shows that you are currently viewing the Pictures folder.

The Pictures folder has two folders nested inside, as displayed in the View pane.

The Folders pane also displays the nested folders.

HANDS-ON 7.2 Create Folders on Your Flash Drive

In this exercise, you will create two new folders on your USB flash drive.

1. Connect your USB flash drive to a USB port.

   Wait a moment for the computer to recognize the USB flash drive. Depending on your USB flash drive, a "tap to choose..." message may appear in the bottom-right corner of the screen. Ignore it, and it will disappear after a few moments.

2. Choose **Start→File Explorer**.

3. Click your **USB flash drive**.

Windows displays the contents of your USB flash drive. Notice the drive name and letter in the address bar path. (Your name and drive letter will probably differ from what's shown here.)

Create a New Folder

Now that you have navigated to your USB flash drive, you are ready to create folders on it. The New Folder command always creates the new folder at your current location.

4. Follow these steps to create and name a new folder:

Ⓐ Choose **Home→New→New Folder**.

Ⓑ Notice the new folder in the View pane. The folder name is highlighted, ready for you to give it a new name.

Ⓒ Type **Photos** to replace the temporary name New Folder and tap Enter.

5. Double-click the new **Photos** folder to open it.

   The folder is empty, so nothing displays in the View pane.

6. Click the **Back** ← button.

   The View pane displays the contents of your USB flash drive. The Photos folder has moved to the top of the list, and this is because Windows normally displays folders before any files.

Create an Additional Folder

7. Choose **Home→New→New Folder**.

8. Name the new folder **USB Documents** and tap Enter .

Moving and Copying Folders and Files

From time to time you may want to reorganize your folders and files. You can easily move folders and files to a new location or put copies of folders or files in other locations.

The Cut, Copy, and Paste Method

To cut and paste or copy and paste folders and files, you use methods similar to those used for text and objects in Chapter 4, Working with Apps. Take time to compare the similarities and differences. As with text, you must select at least one folder or file before you can give the Cut or Copy command. You will learn how to select more than one folder or file at a time later in this chapter.

The Cut, Copy, and Paste commands are conveniently located on the Home tab in the Clipboard group.

How the Commands Work

The following applies to folders and files being cut or copied and then pasted within a folder window:

- **Cut:** Deletes the selected file/folder from its present location only *after* a copy of that file/folder is pasted into a new location.

- **Copy:** Leaves the selected file/folder in its present location when a copy is pasted into a new location.

- **Paste:** Inserts a copy of the last file/folder that was cut or copied into the folder/drive currently open.

- **Undo:** Reverses your most recent Paste command.

FROM THE KEYBOARD

Ctrl + X   Cut selected item

Ctrl + C   Copy selected item

Ctrl + V   Paste

Ctrl + Z   Undo

More About the Paste Command

A few additional features of the Paste command are useful to know:

- You can paste only once if you cut a file or folder.

- You can paste more than once if you copy a file or folder.

- You can usually use the Undo command if you paste a file or folder into an incorrect location.

QUICK REFERENCE: Using Cut, Copy, and Paste with Files/Folders

Task	Procedure
Move folders/files with Cut and Paste	<ul><li>Select the folder/file to move and choose Home→Clipboard→Cut.</li><li>Move to the new location (the Desktop, a folder, or a drive) and choose Home→Clipboard→Paste.</li></ul>
Copy folders/files with Copy and Paste	<ul><li>Select the folder/file to copy and choose Home→Clipboard→Copy.</li><li>Move to the new location (the Desktop, a folder, or a drive) and choose Home→Clipboard→Paste.</li></ul>
Undo a Paste command	<ul><li>After pasting in error, immediately choose Undo from the Quick Access toolbar.</li></ul>

HANDS-ON 7.3 Organize Folders Using Cut, Copy, and Paste

In this exercise, you will copy a file, paste the copy into a different location, and move a file using Cut and Paste.

Before You Begin: You will be using folders created earlier in this chapter as well as files you saved in Chapter 4: Working with Apps. Your flash drive should still be connected.

1. Start **File Explorer** and click on your **USB flash drive**.

2. Follow these steps to copy a file into a folder:

Photos   USB Documents

image4   my signature

   ⓐ Click the **my signature** file to select it and then choose **Home→Clipboard→ Copy**.

   ⓑ Double-click the **USB Documents** folder to open it and then choose **Paste** from the Ribbon.

3. Click the **Back** ← button on the toolbar.

   Windows moves you out of the folder, back to viewing your USB flash drive. The original my signature file is still on the drive.

4. Double-click the **USB Documents** folder to reopen it.

5. Select the **my signature** file.

6. Choose **Home→Organize→Delete**.

7. From the Delete File prompt that appears, choose **Yes**.

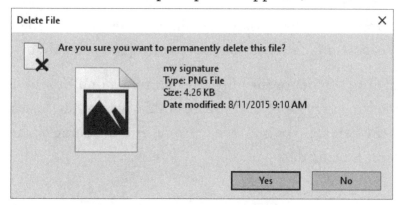

8. Click the **Back** button to view your USB flash drive window.

   The original My Signature file is still on the drive.

Cut and Paste Method

9. Click the **My Signature** file and then choose **Home→Clipboard→Cut**.

10. Double-click the **USB Documents folder** to open it.

11. Choose **Home→Clipboard→Paste**.

12. Click the **Back** button on the toolbar to return to the drive window.

    The My Signature file is no longer on the drive; it has been moved.

13. Click **Customize Quick Access Toolbar** and choose **Undo** �**⤺** from the menu.

   This adds an Undo ↩ *button to the Quick Access toolbar.*

14. Click **Undo** ↩ on the Quick Access toolbar.

    The My Signature file is returned to the drive because the Cut command has been undone.

The Drag-and-Drop Method

You used drag and drop in Chapter 5, Using Email, to move emails to folders. Folders and files in the same locations can easily be moved or copied using drag and drop.

When you drag and drop a folder or file onto another folder or different drive, Windows does something very helpful. If you hesitate over the new location, a ScreenTip displays the default action (Move or Copy) and the name of the folder or drive where the object is being dropped.

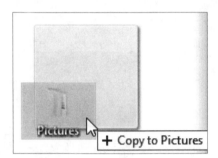

Although the left mouse button can be used to drag, it's better for new users to use the right mouse button when dragging and dropping folders/files, because the right mouse button gives you more control over what will happen when you drop the folder or file. Using the right mouse button displays a menu when you release the button that allows you to choose a command to complete the procedure.

If you drop in this location with the left mouse button, the default command (in bold) occurs.

You also have the option of cancelling the procedure.

Using the right mouse button to drag and drop something to a new location lets you choose Copy Here or Move Here from a pop-up menu.

Tip! Develop good habits. Use the right mouse button to drag and drop because it gives you more control over the procedure and makes you less likely to make mistakes.

HANDS-ON 7.4 Copy and Move Files Using Drag and Drop

In this exercise, you will use your right mouse button with drag and drop to copy and move a file to another location on your USB flash drive.

1. Follow these steps to move and copy files using both drag and drop and the right mouse button:

   A Place your mouse pointer over **my signature**, hold down the right (not left) mouse button and drag over the **USB Documents** folder, and then release the mouse button.

   B Choose **Copy Here** from the pop-up menu.

   The my signature file is still on the drive window.

2. Double-click to open the **USB Documents** folder.

   Notice that a copy of the my signature file is now in the folder.

3. Select the **my signature** file and choose **Home→Organize→Delete**.

4. From the Delete File prompt that appears, choose **Yes**.

5. Click the **Back** ← button.

Move a File Using Drag and Drop

6. Using the right mouse button, drag the **my signature** file onto the **USB Documents** folder and release the mouse button.

   A pop-up menu appears, asking what you want to do with the file.

7. Choose **Move Here** from the pop-up menu.

   The my signature file disappears from view because it has been moved into a folder.

8. Double-click the **USB Documents** folder to open it.

   The my signature file is there, as you would expect.

9. Click the **Back** ← button.

10. Choose **Undo** from the Quick Access toolbar.

The my signature file reappears in the USB flash drive view because the Move Here command was undone.

. . . .

Selecting Multiple Files

You can select more than one folder or file at a time. When you select multiple folders or files, Windows lets you move or copy the whole group at the same time, which can save you a lot of time. It can also prevent you from making errors or forgetting files, which can happen if you move files one at a time.

QUICK REFERENCE: Selecting Multiple Folders and Files

Task	Procedure
Select multiple contiguous folders/files	▪ Click the first folder/file. ▪ Hold down Shift, click the last folder/file in the group, and then release Shift. Note: Add additional folders/files to the selection by holding down Ctrl and clicking the desired items.
Select multiple noncontiguous folders/files	▪ Hold down Ctrl and then click each folder/file you wish to select once. Note: Click a selected item while holding down Ctrl to deselect it.
Select a group of folders/files by dragging	▪ Taking care not to point at any file/folder, place the tip of the mouse pointer below the last file/folder in the group of files/folders you wish to select. ▪ Drag with the left mouse button up and to the left to make a selection box large enough to select the group.
Selecting all folders/files	▪ Choose Home→Select→Select All, or hold down Ctrl and tap A.

HANDS-ON 7.5 Select and Move Multiple Items

In this exercise, you will move multiple items simultaneously using different methods. To begin, you will use the ⎡Ctrl⎤ and ⎡Shift⎤ keys.

1. Follow these steps to select multiple items using the ⎡Shift⎤ key:

Ⓐ Click once (don't double-click) to select the **Photos** folder.

Ⓑ Hold down ⎡Shift⎤, click once on **image2**, and then release ⎡Shift⎤.

Notice that using the ⎡Shift⎤ key selected the contiguous folders and files between the first and last selected items.

2. Follow these steps to select multiple items using the ⎡Ctrl⎤ key:

Ⓐ Click once on the **Photos** folder to deselect all items except Photos.

Ⓑ Hold down ⎡Ctrl⎤ and click **image2** once to select it as well.

Ⓒ While holding down ⎡Ctrl⎤, click **image1** once to add the file to the selection.

Notice that using ⎡Ctrl⎤ lets you select noncontiguous items.

You also can combine the ⎡Shift⎤ and ⎡Ctrl⎤ key methods to select several files with ⎡Shift⎤ and then select or deselect other folders and files with ⎡Ctrl⎤.

Select Multiple Items by Dragging

3. Follow these steps to select multiple items:

Ⓐ Place the mouse pointer under **image2**, hold down the left mouse button, and drag a selection box that touches the **image2** and **image1** icons.

Ⓑ Release the mouse button and notice that both files remain selected.

Move Multiple Files by Dragging

4. With image1 and image2 files still selected, follow these steps to move the multiple selected files:

A Hold your mouse pointer over one of the selected icons, hold down the right mouse button, and drag the files over the **USB Documents** folder (notice the ScreenTip that appears).

B Release the mouse button and choose **Move Here**.

The files disappear from view as they are moved into the folder.

5. Double-click the **USB Documents** folder to open it and confirm that the files have been moved.

6. Close **File Explorer**.

Deleting and Restoring Folders and Files

Windows enables you to clean up your computer folders by deleting unwanted folders and files. Folders and files that are deleted from an internal or external hard drive are moved to the Recycle Bin folder. Folders and files in the Recycle Bin can later be returned to their original locations, if desired.

The Recycle Bin

The Recycle Bin is a unique folder and is important enough that Windows includes an icon linked to it on the Desktop. The Recycle Bin folder serves as a temporary storage place for folders and files deleted from internal hard disk drives.

It is like your recycle bin at home. When you put something into a recycle bin, it stays there unless you change your mind and retrieve it, or until it is permanently removed by the recycling truck. Likewise, folders and files sent to the Recycle Bin folder can be retrieved and sent back to their original locations (restored), but a folder or file that is deleted from the Recycle Bin is permanently deleted.

Warning! If you right-click the Recycle Bin icon on the Desktop and choose Empty Recycle Bin, all of its folders and files will be permanently deleted.

Deleting Folders and Files

Only folders/files deleted from drives categorized by Windows as internal or external hard disk drives are moved to the Recycle Bin. However, folders/files deleted from drives categorized by Windows as devices with removable storage (such as USB flash drives and CD/DVD drives) *are not* moved to the Recycle Bin. These deleted folders and files are permanently deleted and cannot be restored.

Windows will display a Delete Folder dialog box similar to the following if the objects being deleted will not be sent to the Recycle Bin.

Note! USB flash drives normally show up as removable drives. Occasionally some will show up as hard drives. As a precaution, you should always assume that folders/files deleted from USB drives will be permanently deleted.

Restoring Folders and Files

Deleted folders/files moved to the Recycle Bin folder can be restored (moved back) to the original locations from which they were deleted. When the Recycle Bin is opened, there is a Restore All Items button on the Ribbon. The Restore button is used to initiate the restore, but its label will change depending on the number of items selected.

QUICK REFERENCE: Deleting and Restoring Folders and Files

Task	Procedure
Delete a file or folder	▪ Select the folder(s)/file(s) to delete.
	▪ Tap Delete ; choose Yes to confirm the deletion.
Open the Recycle Bin	▪ Double-click the Recycle Bin icon.
Restore items from the Recycle Bin	▪ Open the Recycle Bin.
	▪ If desired, select the item(s) to be restored, using Ctrl or Shift if necessary.
	▪ Choose Recycle Bin Tools→Manage→Restore→Restore All Items or Restore the Selected Items.
Empty the Recycle Bin	▪ Double-click the Recycle Bin icon.
	▪ Choose Recycle Bin Tools→Manage→Manage→Empty Recycle Bin.

Warning! WARNING! All folders and files in the Recycle Bin are permanently deleted when you choose Empty Recycle Bin.

HANDS-ON 7.6 Delete and Restore Folders or Files

In this exercise, you will delete a folder on the Desktop and then restore it.

Before You Begin: If there is not a folder titled Delete Practice on your Desktop, please complete Hands-On 7.1 before continuing.

1. Click the **Delete Practice** folder on the Desktop to select it.

2. Tap the Delete key to delete it.
   Now you will restore the file back to the Desktop.

3. Double-click the **Recycle Bin** icon on the Desktop.

Windows opens a new folder window to display the contents of the Recycle Bin. Depending on what others have done on the computer, the folder may contain just the folder you deleted or many other folders and files as well.

4. Click the **Delete Practice** folder in the Recycle Bin. (You may need to scroll down the list to find it.)

5. Choose **Recycle Bin Tools→Manage→Restore the Selected Items**.

6. **Close** ⌷×⌷ the **Recycle Bin** and confirm that the Delete Practice folder is restored to the Desktop.

OneDrive File Storage

OneDrive uses a simplified file system that is not much more complicated than the one used in Outlook.com. In fact, all of the concepts regarding files and folders that you have learned so far apply to OneDrive.

The biggest difference between OneDrive and your USB flash drive is that OneDrive is on the Internet and available from any of your computers and smartphones, whereas your USB flash drive is a physical item you carry with you.

Once you get used to using OneDrive, you may find that you no longer need to carry a USB flash drive.

Menu bar

Navigation pane   Folders pane

The OneDrive default screen as seen in your browser.

Navigation pane

Menu bar

Folders pane

The default screen from OneDrive on an Android smartphone.

Creating OneDrive Folders

OneDrive enables you to create folders for sorting stored files by using the New button.

The drop-down menu on the New button also allows you to create blank new documents for other free Office Online apps, including Word Online.

HANDS-ON 7.7 Create a OneDrive Folder

In this exercise, you will create a folder in OneDrive.

1. Start **OneDrive**.

2. Click the **New** button on the menu bar and then choose **Folder** from the drop-down menu.

3. In the dialog box that appears, type **Uploaded Files** and click **Create**.

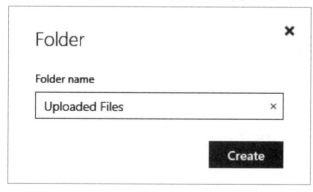

Notice that the folder appears in OneDrive.

4. Click the **Uploaded Files** folder once.
The folder is empty.

5. Create another folder named **Pictures**.
Pictures is now a subfolder of Uploaded Files.

6. Close **OneDrive**.

Navigating Between Folders

OneDrive, like File Explorer, uses a path to show where you are located in OneDrive. In OneDrive, clicking up the path is the easiest way to back out of a subfolder, as OneDrive has no button for going up one folder or a way to jump to the main view of OneDrive.

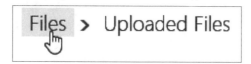

For example, if you are in the Uploaded Files folder and want to move back to the main view of OneDrive, you can click Files in the path.

HANDS-ON 7.8 Move Between Folders

In this exercise, you will move around between folders on OneDrive.

1. Open **OneDrive**.

2. Click the **Uploaded Files** folder.

   Notice that the path shows you are in Uploaded Files.

3. Click the **Pictures** folder.

   Files > Uploaded Files > Pictures

   Notice that the path has grown to show you the Pictures folder.

4. On the path, click **Uploaded Files**.

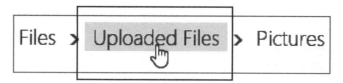

   The path now shows Uploaded Files as the end of the path and your current location.

5. Click **Files**.

   You are now on the main screen of OneDrive.

6. Close **OneDrive**.

Tip! No matter how far down into the path of subfolders you are in, clicking Files in OneDrive will always bring you back to the main screen.

Uploading Files to OneDrive

You can upload files from your computer to OneDrive with the click of a button.

Files uploaded to OneDrive are immediately available to all of your computers and devices. Any file type can be uploaded, including documents, music files, images, and videos.

When uploading, only a copy of the selected file is uploaded. The original is not moved.

Tip! You don't have to worry about file sizes, because recently, OneDrive raised the individual file size limit to 10 gigabytes per file, which is bigger than even a full-length movie file!

HANDS-ON 7.9 Upload to OneDrive

In this exercise, you will upload two files from your USB flash drive to OneDrive.

1. Start **OneDrive** and click the **Uploaded Files** folder. Make sure your USB flash drive is plugged in.

2. Click the **Upload** button on the menu bar.
   An Open dialog box appears.

3. Follow these steps to choose a file to upload:

Ⓐ Choose your **USB flash drive** from the navigation pane.

Ⓑ Choose the **my signature** file in the folder pane.

Ⓒ Click **Open**.

Watch as a message appears on the menu bar, showing that the upload is in progress. When it's complete, a pop-up message appears to let you know.

4. Follow steps 1–3 to upload the **image1** file to the **Uploaded Files** folder.
   Remember, image1 and image2 are now located in the USB Documents folder on your USB flash drive. Leave OneDrive open.

Downloading from OneDrive

Any files you have stored on OneDrive can be downloaded (copied) to your computer or device for use.

To download, you first need to select the file. OneDrive enables you to do this via a small round checkbox.

Selecting Letter from Sylvia for download using the round checkbox

By default, files downloaded from OneDrive using the Edge browser are put into the Downloads folder on your PC. Other browsers may download to a different location.

The ability to upload and download files enables you to have maximum flexibility when working with files. For example, you could create a file on a school computer, upload it to OneDrive, work on it from your smartphone on your bus ride home, and then download it to your laptop for final editing on your full version of Microsoft Word.

HANDS-ON 7.10 Download from OneDrive

In this exercise, you will download the Letter from Sylvia from OneDrive to your computer.

1. Put your mouse pointer over the **Letter from Sylvia** and then click in the round checkbox that appears.

2. Click **Download** on the menu bar.
   The combination of OneDrive and the Edge browser has placed a copy of your file in the Downloads folder on your computer.

3. Close any messages that appear along the bottom of the screen.

4. Close **OneDrive** and then open **File Explorer**.

5. In the Frequent Folders section under Quick Access, double-click **Downloads**.

You should see the Letter from Sylvia.

6. Close **File Explorer**.

. . . .

Concepts Review

To check your knowledge of the key concepts introduced in this chapter, complete the Concepts Review quiz on this page. Or, you can take the quiz online by going to **labyrinthelab/wtcb10**.

Page number

1. The rules for naming folders are the same as those for naming files. **true** **false** _____

2. You can use the Cut and Paste commands to move folders/files from one location to another. **true** **false** _____

3. Deleted folders/files are always moved to the Recycle Bin. **true** **false** _____

4. If you delete a picture from the Desktop and then restore it, Windows restores it to the My Pictures folder. **true** **false** _____

5. Folders and files deleted from a USB flash drive are not placed in the Recycle Bin. **true** **false** _____

6. Files stored on OneDrive can be accessed on any computer or device. **true** **false** _____

7. You can create new folders _____.

   a. in an existing folder

   b. on a drive

   c. on the Desktop

   d. All of the above

   Page number: _____

8. The Recycle Bin _____.

   a. includes an icon on the Desktop

   b. serves as a temporary holding area for deleted files and folders

   c. holds files and folders until they are permanently deleted or removed from the Recycle Bin

   d. All of the above

   Page number: _____

9. Multiple files and folders can be selected by _____.

   a. clicking them with Shift held

   b. clicking them with Ctrl held

   c. dragging across files/folders

   d. All of the above

   Page number: _____

10. One advantage of using OneDrive instead of a USB flash drive is _____.

   a. your OneDrive account has more storage space than your laptop

   b. OneDrive is available even with no Internet connection

   c. files are immediately available to all devices, including your smartphone

   d. None of the above

   Page number: _____

SKILL BUILDER 7.1 Find and Copy Files

In this exercise, you will use the drag-and-drop method to move files into folders on OneDrive.

1. Open **OneDrive**.

2. Choose **New→Folder**.

3. Type **Letters** and then click **Create**.

4. Click and drag **Letter from Sylvia** onto the new **Letters** folder.

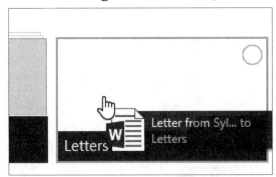

Notice that your mouse cursor shows your file being carried.

5. Click and drag **Office Manager Letter** to the **Letters** folder.

The Letters folder now shows it has two files in it.

6. Click the **Letters** folder to view its contents.

Files > Letters

Letter from Sylvia

Office Manager Letter

SKILL BUILDER 7.2 Open a File Directly from OneDrive

In this exercise, you will open a Word document directly from OneDrive and view it in Word Online.

1. Click the **Office Manager Letter**.

   Word Online automatically opens the document in preview mode.

2. From the menu bar, choose **Edit Document→Edit in Word Online**.

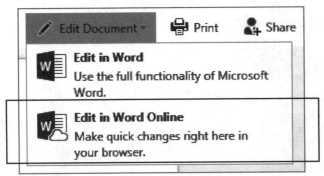

   Notice that you can also choose to open and edit the file in Word on your computer, if installed. Since Word Online was chosen, it is open, and your document is ready for editing.

3. Change *Sincerely* at the end of the letter to **Thank you**.

   Word Online saves your document as you work.

4. Close **Word Online** and **OneDrive**.

SKILL BUILDER 7.3 Create a File and Upload to OneDrive

When you are working on a project and intend to store files on OneDrive for easy access from anywhere, you may find that creating basic documents ahead of time helps you get organized. For example, you might create one file to hold the project description, another file to hold random notes, and another file to list citations and websites used for your research. In this exercise, you will create a basic file on your Desktop and upload it to OneDrive.

1. Right-click the **Desktop** and choose **New→Text Document**.

A blank document appears on your Desktop.

2. Type **Research Notes** and press ⌈Enter⌋.

Notice that the default name of the file is replaced by your text.

3. Double-click the **Research Notes** file to open it.

4. Type **Research Notes**.

5. Choose **File→Save**.

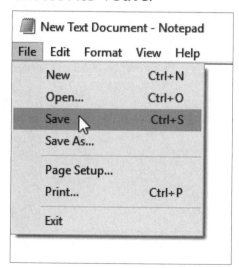

6. Close the file.

7. Start **OneDrive**.

8. Click the **Uploaded Files** folder.

9. Follow these steps to upload the Research Notes file:

Ⓐ Choose **Desktop** from the navigation pane.

Ⓑ Click **Research Notes**.

Ⓒ Click **Open**.

10. Close **OneDrive** after the upload is complete.

UNIT 3: THE INTERNET AND MORE

In the first two chapters in this unit, you will learn how to connect to, use, perform searches in, create Web Notes in, and protect yourself from threats when using the Internet and, in particular, Microsoft's Edge browser. You will find that the Internet allows you to access information, pictures, movies, music, games, and much more. In Chapter 10, you will learn more about Cortana, Microsoft's personal digital assistant; adjusting the settings on your computer; how to keep your apps up to date; and how to use Microsoft's Store.

CHAPTER 8

Using the Internet

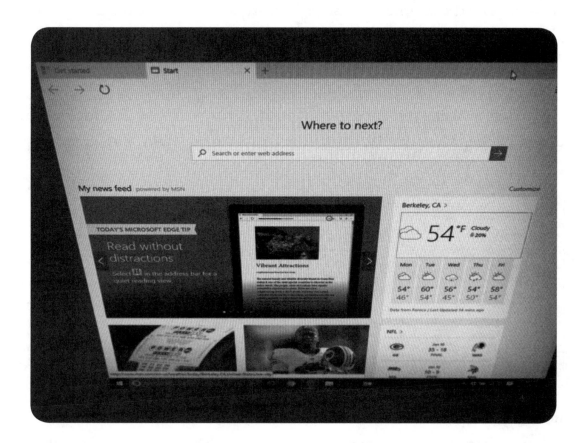

LEARNING OBJECTIVES

- Use a World Wide Web address to go directly to a website
- Identify the main components of a web address
- Use Microsoft Edge to browse the web
- Create a favorite with Microsoft Edge
- Use the Hub in Microsoft Edge

Connecting to the Internet has become one of the primary reasons for owning a computer and learning to use computer technology. The Internet provides you with access to a wealth of information on almost any topic; entertainment, pictures, movies, music, and games; and the ability to shop the world from your home. In this chapter, you will use Microsoft Edge to browse the web.

Learning Resources: **labyrinthelab.com/wtcb10**

📂 Case Study: Browsing on the Web

Patrick is planning a trip to Arizona and figures most of the information he needs is available on the Internet. He uses Microsoft Edge to browse the Internet and searches using the term *grand canyon*.

🔍 grand canyon	→

He finds an amazing amount of information. Fortunately, the first page listed is the official National Park Service site for the Grand Canyon (www.nps.gov/grca).

Grand Canyon National Park - Official Site
www.nps.gov/grca/index.htm ▾
Mar 26, 2015 · **Grand Canyon National Park**. A powerful and inspiring landscape, **Grand Canyon** overwhelms our senses through its immense size. Unique ...

Lodging
Canyon Squire Inn (928) 638-2681:
Grand Canyon Suites (928) 638 ...

Directions
Where is **Grand Canyon**? **Grand Canyon** is in the northwest corner ...

Maps
Grand Canyon Area Map (2.5 MB PDF File) revised 2/2015 Shows ...

Fees and Reservations
Entrance Fees. Admission to **Grand Canyon National Park** is for ...

Plan Your Visit
Drier and Warmer - Then a Chance of Showers and Thunderstorms ...

Weather/Road Conditions
South Rim **Grand Canyon National Park**. Updated: Friday, May 22, ...

See results only from nps.gov

The National Park Service web page has information on everything Patrick needs: hotels, restaurants, events, and things to do. There are links to make reservations, helpful information, maps, and beautiful pictures. This site is going to make planning his trip easier, so he adds the web page to his favorites.

The Internet

The Internet has been in existence for more than 40 years. In its infancy, it was text based and was used primarily by the military and educational institutions. Using the Internet often involved typing long strings of text on a black screen (see the following illustration). That changed in the early 1990s, with the creation of the World Wide Web. The World Wide Web simplifies access to information through an interface that includes colored graphics and point-and-click links. Users don't have to remember and type complex addresses or know specifically where information is located; they can just point and click on links or onscreen buttons to jump to the information. This makes the Internet easier to use, more colorful, and more interesting.

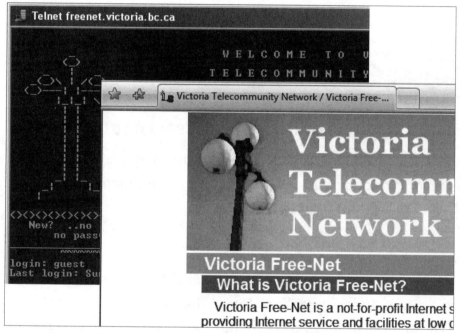

This is Victoria Free-Net accessed using an older, text-based technology (Telnet, top left) and with a newer graphical browser technology (Internet Explorer, bottom right).

The World Wide Web

By far the most dominant segment of the Internet is the World Wide Web (WWW), commonly referred to as the **web**. The web is only one of many technology pieces that make up the Internet, but it has become the most commonly used because of its simplicity and graphic features.

Today's web pages have colorful multimedia displays and easy-to-click links to other web pages. Most people can access the web by learning some simple skills and understanding a few basic concepts.

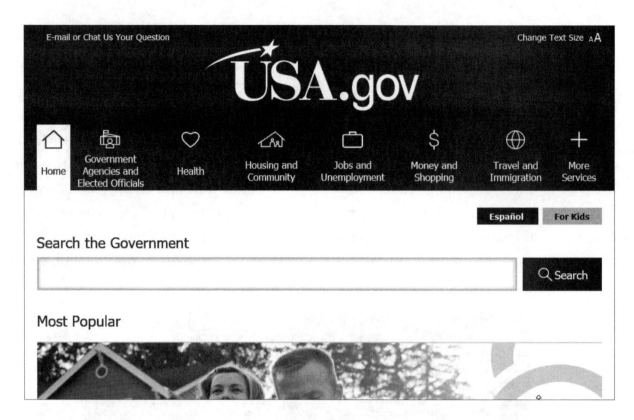

Equipment Used to Connect to the Internet

You need specific equipment to connect to the Internet. New computers typically include most of the equipment needed, but some equipment may be provided to you by your **Internet service provider (ISP)**.

Modems

A *modem* (stands for **mod**ulate/**dem**odulate) enables your computer to connect to the Internet via a standard telephone line. A dial-up modem converts the analog signals of the phone system into the digital signal your computer uses. Once connected to a phone line, your computer can dial the phone number of your ISP to gain access to the Internet. Dial-up modem connections are slow compared to the high-speed connection options available in most parts of the country today, and they are used when other options are not available.

A high-speed modem converts the signals sent over telephone lines, over cable lines, or from a satellite into signals your computer can use to communicate with the Internet. It is called a high-speed modem because it moves data to and from your computer at a much faster rate than a conventional dial-up modem.

Routers

Once you have an Internet connection, a **router** enables you to connect multiple computers to that connection. A typical router will allow four computers to be networked together with network cables so they can all access the Internet.

A common Motorola cable modem and router

A wireless router works just like a regular router, with the added benefit of allowing access to the Internet via a wireless connection. Most laptop computers now have wireless capability; they can connect wirelessly at home or other locations that make their wireless routers available to the public, such as coffee shops, restaurants, and hotels. Many routers now combine the modem, router, and wireless router into one unit.

In infrastructure mode, a router or access point handles all network traffic.

New technologies for connecting to the Internet emerge all the time. How Internet service is delivered keeps changing, most recently with the advent of WiMAX and smartphone-based Internet. The way the service is used also changes, and now it is being accessed from more portable devices such as cell phones and laptops, but you may soon access it from your watch or glasses.

Connection Types

Connection to the Internet is made possible through a business known as an ISP (Internet service provider). Connecting to a service provider can be accomplished in several ways:

- via a telephone line using a dial-up modem

- via a telephone line using a high-speed modem (DSL)

- via a TV cable using a high-speed modem

- via a network at work or school

- via wireless connections, such as satellites, cell towers, and dish systems

Internet Service Providers

An ISP provides the connection between you and the Internet. The ISP is usually paid a monthly fee to maintain your connection. Many ISPs provide other services as well, and they might provide Internet services as part of a bundle of multiple services.

Most people now get their Internet connection from their cable or phone provider. That wasn't always the case. In the early days of the Internet, many ISPs were local businesses run by technology people. Some users are opting to return to local small businesses over large corporations, much in the same way they choose independent, local shops for their groceries, home goods, and other items. To find a local ISP, do a web search!

In most cases, the ISP will provide you with software that will automatically configure your computer with the correct settings for your new Internet connection as well as instructions for setting up any needed equipment.

Dial-Up Connections

A dial-up connection was the first type of Internet connection available to home consumers. It uses a dial-up modem and a standard phone line (sometimes referred to as POTS, for "plain old telephone system"). Dial-up gets its name from the fact that special software in your computer has to dial a phone number to make the connection.

High-Speed Connections

High-speed is a generic term for services that provide information transfer rates that are higher than typical dial-up transfer rates. You can access high-speed connections through your TV cable, phone line (referred to as digital subscriber line, or DSL), or even satellite dish.

High-speed connections can be more than 100 times faster than dial-up connections. This means that a document that would take you 20 minutes to download over a dial-up connection might take only a few seconds with a high-speed connection.

Network Connections

When you use a computer at work or school, you are connected to the Internet through a network. Connection to the Internet through a network allows you to move more data at a higher speed (more **bandwidth**) and to share that information with many computers at the same time. The Internet itself is a network of networks.

Wireless Connections

Wireless connections have become popular for an obvious reason—there is no wire. That means you do not have to be tied to a desk; you can be mobile and still be connected to the Internet.

Connection Speeds

Connections are measured in kilobits per second. High-speed connections may reference their speed in megabits. One megabit equals 1,000 kilobits.

Connection type	Speed	Example
Dial-up connection	56 kilobits	■ 5–7 seconds to view an average web page ■ 20–30 minutes to download one song
High-speed connection	20–200 megabits	■ 1–2 seconds to view an average web page ■ 15–20 seconds to download a song ■ Less than 30 minutes to download a movie

Web Browsers

Once you're connected to the web, you need a web **browser** to explore it. The web is like a very large coffee table book—it contains millions of pages filled with vibrant pictures, text, videos, and sounds on any topic you can think of. The browser lets you explore this "book," by jumping from page to page using special text and graphics that link you to other pages. There are many different browsers, and you can choose the one you want to use. You may also have more than one browser on your computer or device.

Microsoft Edge

The exercises in this book use Microsoft Edge, which is Microsoft's newest browser and replaces Internet Explorer as the default browser for Microsoft. Edge comes installed on all versions of Windows 10. You have already used the Edge browser in previous chapters for accessing OneDrive and Outlook.com.

 You will notice that the Edge icon looks a lot like the Explorer icon. Microsoft did this on purpose to show the heritage of Edge and to ease the transition for those individuals who have used Explorer for many years.

Internet Explorer

Internet Explorer was one of the dominant browsers for many years and has been the browser of choice for many schools and corporations. You will find Internet Explorer on most PCs, as it was the default browser for Windows up to version 8.1.

Chrome

One of the dominant browsers available, Chrome was created by Google and is very popular among Google fans. Chrome is available at www.google.com/chrome.

Firefox

One of the most popular alternatives, Firefox is a free browser that you can download and use on your Windows 10 computer. Firefox is available at www.mozilla.com.

Other Browsers

There are dozens of other browsers available on the Internet, including browsers that have specific functions or browsers that work on specific devices or smartphones. Other browsers you may hear mentioned include:

- Safari

- Opera

- Opera Mini

- Android's browser

One of the great features of the Internet is the ability to explore and discover many new pieces of software and various ways to accomplish the digital tasks you need to complete.

Uniform Resource Locators (URLs)

In order for a browser to find specific websites, there needs to be a way to uniquely identify them. Every site on the Internet has a **Uniform Resource Locator (URL)**, which is also referred to as an address. You use the address to find and display a particular website (location). It's similar to finding a house by looking for its unique address, and just like houses, no two websites can have the same address.

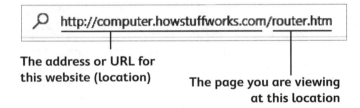

The address or URL for this website (location)

The page you are viewing at this location

Top-Level Domains

Website addresses are divided into major **domains**. The original domains were used to divide Internet addresses into groups of websites with a common purpose. These six domains are used mainly by American websites, because the US government was their creator and manager. As the web has gotten more popular, more and more foreign websites are using these major domains because of their global commercial success. The domain appears at the end of a web address.

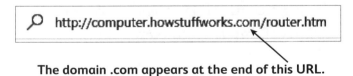

The domain .com appears at the end of this URL.

THE ORIGINAL TOP-LEVEL DOMAINS

Top-Level Domain	Designation	Notes
.com	Commercial	The most commonly used domain, open to any business, organization, or individual.
.edu	Education	Used by educational institutions, such as schools and colleges. There are special requirements for groups wanting to use this domain.
.gov	Government	Federal, state, and local government websites have this domain. It ensures that the information you are viewing is official government information, something that can be hard to tell with some .com websites.
.org	Organization	This domain was once reserved for nonprofit organizations, but today anybody can register for .org names.
.net	Internet	In times past, this domain was used mostly for Internet-related companies, but as businesses have increasingly had trouble finding good web addresses ending in .com, they have turned to .net.
.mil	Military	One of the least used domains on the Internet; reserved for the American military. Why does the military get their own top-level domain? The early research that created the Internet was funded by the Advance Research Projects Agency, ARPA.

These original top-level domains were the only ones used for over twenty years. In the last few years, though, a flood of new domain names have been created. As of February of 2015, there were more than one thousand top-level domains. A complete list of top-level domains, including recently added domains, can be found at http://en.wikipedia.org/wiki/List_of_Internet_top-level_domains.

Country Codes

Country codes also are top-level domains and consist of two-letter abbreviations that appear at the end of an address. Every country in the world has been assigned a country code that can be used in the creation of web addresses. Although addresses with country codes are not as common, you will find more of them as you research outside commercial and American websites.

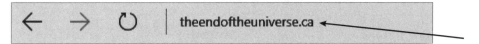

This web address ends in .ca, which is the country code for Canada.

SOME COMMON COUNTRY CODES

Country	Code	Country	Code
United States	.us	Canada	.ca
England	.uk	Japan	.jp
Mexico	.mx	France	.fr
Iraq	.iq	Russia	.ru
Antarctica	.aq	Cuba	.cu

Basic Navigation

Let's explore how Microsoft Edge enables you to navigate the web. With some basic buttons and commands, you can move from location to location.

- **Address bar:** The address bar is where you enter the address of a web page or website.

- **Back and Forward buttons:** The Back button takes you back to previously viewed web pages while the Forward button returns you to more recently viewed web pages.

- **Refresh button:** Some web pages have content that changes frequently (such as an auction site). The Refresh button enables you to reload the page without having to type the address in the address bar again. The Refresh button replaces the Stop button once a web page has loaded.

- **Stop button:** This button stops a page from loading. If a web page is taking too long to load, clicking the Stop button will stop the loading process. This enables you to type in a new address or click the Refresh button to try loading the page again.

Stop button

Back and Forward buttons

Refresh button

Address bar

google.com/?gws_rd=ssl

Hyperlinks

A **hyperlink**, or "link," is text or a picture that is linked to another page on the web. If you think of the web as a giant book, these links allow you to instantly jump from one page to another in the book.

Typically, text links will be underlined and blue in color. On occasion, you will find text links that are in a color other than blue. Picture links can look like a normal image or be designed to look like buttons.

When your mouse cursor is over a picture or text link, it will turn into a small hand with a pointing finger. When you click the mouse, you will be taken to whatever page that link points to.

Once you reach a web page or a website, you can move to other web pages or websites (or the website's other pages) by clicking the hyperlinks.

When your mouse pointer is over a link in a web page, the pointer turns into a small hand.

Tip!   Webpage, web page, and page are all used interchangeably to describe a web page on the Internet. In this book, we use the two-word form: web page.

HANDS-ON 8.1 Navigate to a Web Page

In this exercise, you will enter the address for Google News and use the Back button to navigate.

1. Start **Edge**.

2. Click next to the Refresh button to make the address bar appear.

The address bar is hidden in the Microsoft Edge browser until you click in this area.

3. Click in the address bar, type **news.google.com** as shown, and tap Enter.

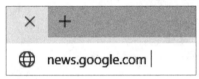

4. Use the **Back** ← button to return to the Edge start page.

. . . .

Tabbed Browsing

One of the features in most browsers is tabbed browsing. This feature enables you to have multiple web pages open at the same time. Each web page has a tab (like a recipe card), making it easy to flip through your open web pages.

This feature comes in handy when you are doing research, because you can have multiple sources open at the same time and quickly jump back and forth among them by clicking the tabs. It's also a great way to scan news headlines because it enables you to have multiple newspaper websites open simultaneously.

Tip! Tabbed browsing is particularly useful when your Internet connection is running slowly; as one page is loading, you can be reading another.

The busy symbol appears while the web page is loading. Even with a high-speed connection, you may have to wait for a page to load because of congestion on the web or the popularity of a website.

This image shows Edge with three web pages open on different tabs. The first is still loading and displays the system busy symbol.

HANDS-ON 8.2 Use Tabbed Browsing

In this exercise, you will open two web pages within Microsoft Edge.

1. Click next to the Refresh button to make the address page appear.

2. Click in the address bar, type **news.google.com**, and tap Enter .

3. Click the small plus button to the right of the larger tab labeled Google News.

A new tab is created.

4. Click next to the Refresh button to make the address bar appear.

5. Click in the address bar, type **cnn.com**, and tap Enter .

Microsoft Edge opens the CNN web page and displays the name in the new web page tab. You should now have two tabs open.

6. Click the **Google News** tab.
   You jump back to Google News.

7. Click the **CNN.com** news tab.
   The browser's view switches back to CNN.

8. Click the **Google News** tab.

9. Close the **Google News** tab.

The Google News tab closes while the CNN tab remains displayed.

10. Close **Edge**.

. . . .

Working with the Hub

The **Hub** is where Edge keeps everything that you collect from the Internet. The Hub is accessed via a button on the right side of the menu bar, and it opens a pane with more information on it.

Items in the hub include (from left to right) Favorites, Reading List, History, and Downloads. Each item in the Hub remembers a specific type of item from the Internet so that you can go back to it at a later time. Each item type is accessed from a button within the Hub.

 HANDS-ON 8.3 Open the Hub

In this exercise, you will open the Hub.

1. Start **Edge**.

2. Click the **Hub** button on the right side of the menu bar.

3. Watch as the Hub slides out of the right side of the Edge screen to display more information.

4. Click the tabs for **Reading List**, **History**, and **Downloads**.

5. Click the **Hub** button again to close the Hub.

6. Close **Edge**.

. . . .

Printing a Web Page

Web pages can be printed if you need a paper copy. Unlike printing a document in Word Online, you may find that web pages don't always print the way you would expect them to. This is because web pages are designed to look good on screen, and the layout technology used to do that makes the printed-out document look slightly different. A web page also has menus, ads, and other visual tools that get printed with the document.

 Sometimes a web page will have a Print button. Whenever possible, use that button, because most of the time the Print button will print a page without all the menus and other visual tools that make the web page print incorrectly.

Tip! A web page can be much longer than a standard page. Make sure to scroll to the bottom of a web page to get an idea of how long the "page" is before you print it.

 HANDS-ON 8.4 Print a Web Page

In this exercise, you will go through the steps to print a web page, but you'll cancel the printing and not actually print the web page so as not to waste paper.

1. Open **Edge**.

2. Type **nps.gov/grca/index.htm** in the address bar and press ⌷Enter⌷.

3. Close any pop-up messages that appear.

4. Click the **More Actions** button on the right-hand side of the menu bar and choose **Print** from the menu.

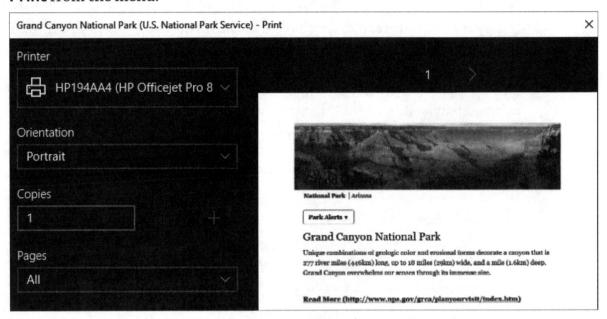

On the left side of the screen, notice that many of the page setup options are the same as those available in Word Online.

5. Click the **Next** arrow on top of the preview and view the various pages.

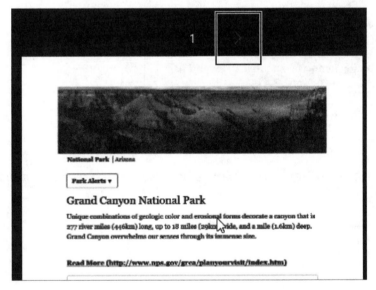

Notice how the printed pages look nothing like the web page you are viewing.

6. Click **Cancel** at the bottom of the Print dialog box.

7. Close **Edge**.

Favorites

A **favorite** is a link to a web page that you save in your browser. A favorite makes it easy for you to return to a web page in the future. Edge gives you the ability to remember numerous addresses in its list of favorites.

When you make a website a favorite, you do not have to remember its address or accurately type it in the address bar every time you want to visit the site. You simply access it from the Favorites center in the Hub.

Favorites center tab   **Folders to organize favorites**

Favorites (links to websites)

Tip!   Not all browsers use the term "favorites." Some browsers, such as Firefox, use the term "bookmark" instead.

FROM THE KEYBOARD

HANDS-ON 8.5 Create a Favorite

In this exercise, you will create a favorite in Edge.

1. Open **Edge**.

2. Click in the address bar, type **google.com**, and tap Enter.

3. Click the **Add to Favorites** ☆ button.

4. Follow these steps to name your favorite:

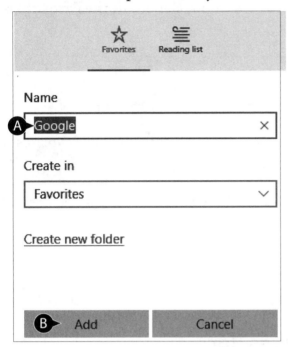

Ⓐ The default name is selected; if necessary, type **Google** to replace it. The default name may not always be descriptive enough and can be changed.

Ⓑ Click **Add**.

Your link to Google has been added to the Favorites center.

5. Click the **Hub** button.

Notice that your link is now in Favorites.

6. Close **Edge**.

Favorites Bar

When enabled, the Favorites Bar displays the favorites of your choice just under the menu bar at the top of the Edge browser window. Generally, the Favorites Bar is used for favorites that you use all the time.

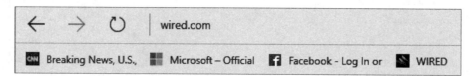

For example, you could put OneDrive and Outlook.com on your Favorites Bar, making it easier to access for this class.

 The Favorites button will be a solid gold color when an address in the address bar is already in the Favorites folder.

HANDS-ON 8.6 Enable the Favorites Bar

In this exercise, you will turn on the Favorites Bar and add favorites to the Favorites Bar folder.

1. Start **Edge**.

2. Click the **More Actions** button on the menu bar and then choose **Settings**.

3. On the Settings menu, click the **Show the Favorites Bar** switch to turn it on.

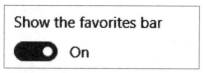

4. Click the **Edge** title bar to close the Settings screen.

5. In the address bar, type **onedrive.com** and press Enter.

6. Click the **Add to Favorites** ☆ button.

7. Follow these steps to add OneDrive to the Favorites Bar:

Ⓐ Change the name of the favorite to **OneDrive**.

Ⓑ From the Create In menu, choose **Favorites Bar**.

Ⓒ Click **Add**.

8. Watch as the OneDrive favorite is added to the Favorites Bar at the top of the Edge browser.

9. Repeat steps 5–9 to add **Outlook.com** to the Favorites Bar.

10. Close **Edge**.

. . . .

Creating Folders in Favorites

Like you have done in Outlook.com, OneDrive, and Windows, you can also create folders in the Hub to organize your favorites. New folders can be created as needed when adding favorites or by right-clicking in the Favorites tab in the Hub.

Being able to organize your Favorites is a critical feature. When you first get started, you won't have many, but as time goes on, most people end up with literally hundreds of favorites in their Favorites tab. Without organization, it's difficult to find a saved link when you need it again.

Tip! It's more important to save favorites for web pages that you work hard to find than for popular websites. Popular websites are easy to find again, whereas a specific web page of information that was buried deep within a website is not so easy to find.

HANDS-ON 8.7 Create a Folder to Sort Favorites

In this exercise, you will create a folder to sort your news links into.

1. Start **Edge**.

2. In the address bar, type **cspan.org** and press Enter.

3. Click the **Add to Favorites** button.

4. Click the **Create New Folder** link.

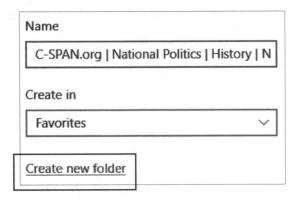

5. Name the folder **News** and then click **Add**.

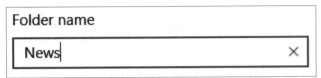

Your favorite is saved in a new folder called News.

6. Click the **Hub** button and then on **News**.

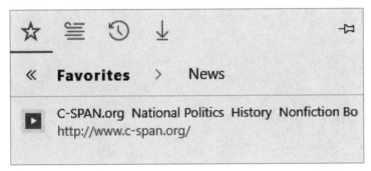

Verify that the C-Span favorite is there.

7. Click on **Favorites** to leave the News folder and return to the main Favorites screen.

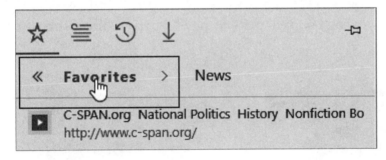

8. Close **Edge**.

. . . .

Removing Favorites

Favorites and folders can be deleted from the Hub. Deleted favorites do not go to the Recycle Bin and cannot be restored.

HANDS-ON 8.8 Remove a Favorite

In this exercise, you will delete a favorite from the Hub.

1. Start **Edge**.

2. In the address bar, type **seattletimes.com** and press Enter .

3. Add this website as a favorite using the default add options.

4. Click the **Hub** button and then right-click on **seattletimes.com** and choose **Delete**.

5. Click the **Hub** button to close the Hub.

6. Close **Edge**.

Reading View

Reading view is a minimalist view that can be used with certain articles that you read on the Internet. If a web page supports Reading view, the icon will show turning pages and darken.

A web page without Reading view (left) and one with Reading view turned on (right). Notice all the menu bars are turned off and the screen's brightness is reduced.

When clicked, toolbars and excess controls on the page are removed so you can focus on just the text and images.

When you save a Favorite and put it on the Reading List (left), you get a picture from the article along with the saved link (right).

When you save a Reading view page as a Favorite, you can select the Reading List tab to save it on. When you do, the Favorite is saved in Reading view and contains a picture from the article.

Reading view can be helpful when reading long articles, as it reduces the number of distractions and helps you focus on what you are reading. But not all pages work in Reading view, as a web page needs to be designed in a certain way to display correctly.

History

The History tab keeps a list of all the web pages you have viewed. You can go back through the history and click on any link to view that web page.

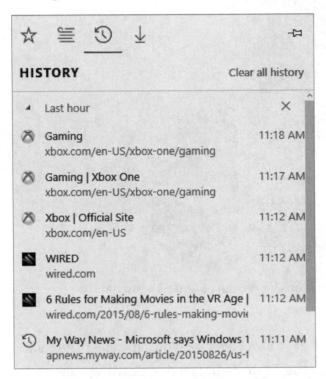

The History tab may also be cleared by using the Clear All History link.

Downloads

The Downloads tab is a list of a files you have downloaded. These are actual files that reside in the Download folder on your computer.

Like the History tab, you can clear this list using the Clear All link.

Concepts Review

To check your knowledge of the key concepts introduced in this chapter, complete the Concepts Review quiz on this page. Or, you can take the quiz online by going to **labyrinthelab/wtcb10**.

Page number

1. Only seven domains are available for use worldwide.   true false _____

2. A router enables only a single computer to connect to a high-speed   true false _____
   Internet connection.

3. Hyperlinks are links to other pages on the web.   true false _____

4. A favorite is a link to a web page saved in your web browser   true false _____
   for later.

5. The Hub connects all your electronic devices in your home.   true false _____

6. The feature in Edge that lets you open multiple web pages in the   true false _____
   same window is called tabbed browsing.

7. Which of the following IS NOT part of the Hub?

   a. Favorites

   b. Reading List

   c. Shopping

   d. Downloads

   Page number: _____

8. Which piece of equipment is used to connect multiple computers to an Internet connection?

   a. modem

   b. phone line

   c. router

   d. network

   Page number: _____

9. The Hub is _____.

   a. where Edge keeps everything that you collect from the Internet

   b. Microsoft's tool for gathering information on your Internet usage

   c. the file management tool for OneDrive

   d. None of the above

   Page number: _____

10. Besides Edge, another web browser is _____.

    a. Internet Explorer

    b. Chrome

    c. Yahoo

    d. Both A and B

    Page number: _____

Skill Builders

SKILL BUILDER 8.1 Create a Favorite

In this exercise, you will create favorites for some popular news sites.

1. Start **Edge**.

2. In the address bar type **cnn.com** and press ⌷Enter⌷.

3. Click the **Add to Favorites** ☆ button and save the link to the **Favorites** folder.

4. Create favorites for **nytimes.com** and **latimes.com**.

5. Click the **Hub** button and verify that the three new favorites are there.
   Notice that the full publication names are listed along with the URL.

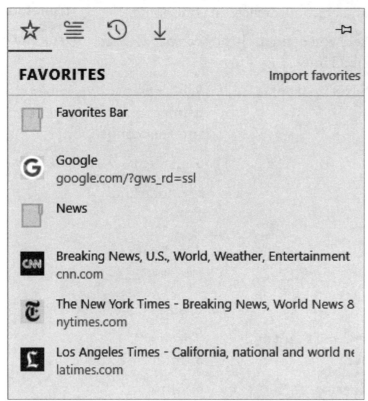

6. Close **Edge**.

SKILL BUILDER 8.2 Drag Favorites to Folders

In this exercise, you will organize your news favorites by dragging them into the News folder.

1. Start **Edge**.

2. Open the **Hub**.

3. Drag the **New York Times** favorite over the **News** folder and release.

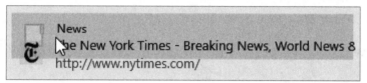

Notice how the entire link is moved by the mouse and placed on top of the News folder.

4. Drag the **Los Angeles Times** favorite into the **News** folder.

5. Click the **News** folder and verify that your links are there. Click **Favorites** on the path to return to the main Favorites tab.

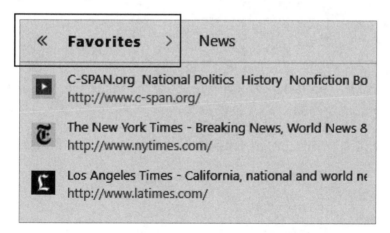

6. Close **Edge**.

SKILL BUILDER 8.3 Move Favorites and Folders

Favorites and folders can be repositioned to better organize your favorites list. In this exercise, you will create a new folder and position it in the Favorites Bar folder.

1. Open **Edge** and then open the **Hub**.

2. Right-click the **News** folder and click **Create New Folder** on the menu that appears.

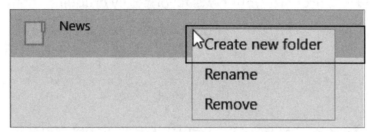

3. Name the new folder `Important Pages` and press Enter.

4. Drag the **Important Pages** folder up under the **Favorites Bar** folder and release.

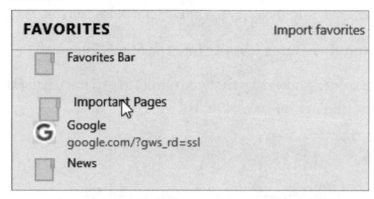

Notice how the other favorites and folders attempt to make room for the folder as you drag across them.

5. Move the **News** folder under the **Important Pages** folder if it isn't already there.

6. Close **Edge**.

Try This at Home

TRY THIS AT HOME 8.1 Download Chrome

You have your choice of many different browsers, and you don't have to use the browser that comes with your computer. In this exercise, you will download Google's Chrome browser and install it on your home computer.

1. Open **Edge**.

2. Type **google.com/chrome** in the address bar and tap Enter.
   This will take you to the download page for Chrome.

2. Click **Download Now**.

3. Remove the checkmark from next to **Set Google Chrome As My Default Browser**, unless you want it to be your default browser.

4. Click **Accept and Install**.

   After a few minutes, the Chrome setup program will finish downloading.

5. Click **Run** on the menu that appears.

ChromeSetup.exe finished downloading.	Run

6. Click **Yes** when asked if you want to allow the app to make changes to your PC.
   It will take a few minutes for Chrome to be installed. A dialog box in the middle of the screen will keep you informed of where you are in the process. After installation, Chrome will automatically open.

7. Look for Google Chrome on your Start menu under "G" for Google Chrome.

Spend some time using Chrome. Many of the things you learned about Edge in this chapter also apply to Chrome.

CHAPTER 9

Researching on the Internet

LEARNING OBJECTIVES

- Use Google to perform a basic search
- Use Google to search for images
- Save Web Notes
- Protect yourself from web threats
- Complete a complicated search

The Internet is a powerful tool for finding information. Access to information grows and expands at an unfathomable pace that was unthinkable to students just a generation ago. In this chapter, you will explore how to search the Internet for various types of information and save notes on web pages with Microsoft Edge. You will also learn how to protect yourself and your computer against web threats.

Learning Resources: **labyrinthelab.com/wtcb10**

📁 Case Study: Web Research

Patrick is still planning his trip to the Grand Canyon. Now that he has his trip basics set, Patrick wants to know more information about the canyon and the area around it. His friend Clarice suggests he use the Google search engine at google.com.

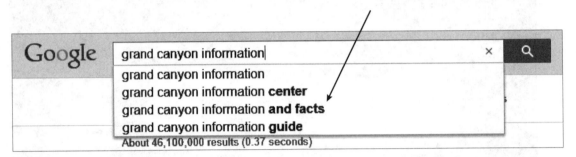

As Patrick starts typing in some search words, he is surprised that Google provides some potential search "strings" as he types. He clicks on a search string titled "grand canyon information and facts," and the search engine returns a list of websites and pages with information and facts about the Grand Canyon.

> **Grand Canyon - Facts & Summary - HISTORY.com**
> www.history.com/topics/**grand-canyon** ▾ History ▾
> Find out more about the history of Grand Canyon, including videos, interesting articles, pictures, historical features and more. Get all the facts on HISTORY.com.
> Videos - Play video The Grand Canyon ... - Creation of Yellowstone

Looking through the results, Patrick finds a page from the History Channel, which he loves! He clicks the link and spends some time learning facts about the Grand Canyon and its history.

Performing a Basic Web Search

Finding information on the web is easy if you know where the information is located and you have a web address (URL) already. When you don't know its location, finding information can be more difficult. Luckily, there are tools called **search engines** that can help you find the information you want from the millions of pages that make up the web.

Search engines are specialized websites that help you find and sort information on the web. Think of a search engine as your own personal web librarian.

How Search Engines Work

Search engines, such as Google, index the web in a way that is similar to how Windows indexes the information on your computer and then uses that index when you use the Search command in a folder window.

Google indexes the web using a vast network of computers around the world that index, or "crawl," the web every few days. When you perform a search, the search engine creates a list of the most relevant web pages it has indexed based on your search words.

Basic Search Techniques

When you search for information on the web using a search engine, it's important to choose the correct words to describe an item. Here are some tips to help you with your searches:

- **Pick a few keywords to describe your search item:** In most cases, three or four words should be enough.

- **Be specific:** If you are interested in books about Windows, using "computer books" to search will display millions of possible web pages, or "hits," but the list will be too broad. You can narrow your search with more specific words, such as "Windows 10 books." This will bring up a shorter list of web pages that are more relevant.

- **Spell your search words correctly:** Misspelled words will generate a list, but it is not likely to be useful.

- **Keep trying:** If you are not finding what you are looking for, add and remove words from your search, and try different words. Even on the web, some subjects can be difficult to find information on. For example, if you are trying to find information on stabilizing riverbanks, "stabilize" and "bank" would be difficult words to use in a search, because you would tend to get mostly financial news related to banking issues. You could try using words such as "stream," "restoration," or "erosion" with the word "river." Sometimes when searching, the quickest way to finding an answer is not the most obvious.

HANDS-ON 9.1 Search with Google

In this exercise, you will perform a basic search using Google. Because the content of the Internet can change rapidly, the information in your search may be slightly different from what is shown on the screen.

1. Start **Edge**.

2. Type **google.com** in the address bar and tap Spacebar + Enter. The space clears any additional characters that may be placed after your text by Edge.

The Google search engine web page appears. Like many search engines, Google works best when you enter three or four words that describe what you are looking for. In this example, you will be looking for information on skiing at Mount Baker.

3. Type the word **mountain** in the Search box.
    Watch how Google switches from a search box in the middle of the screen to one at the top of the screen.

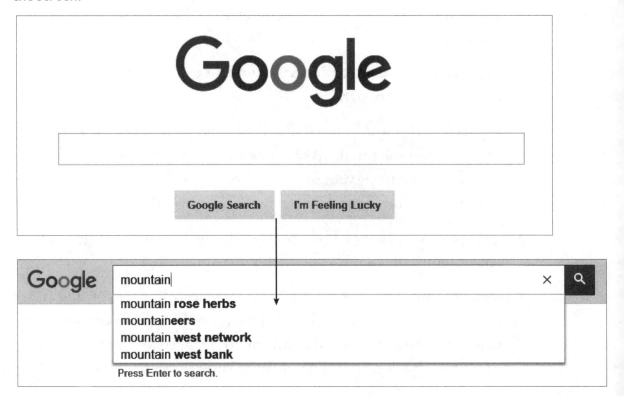

As you type, Google will try to guess what you are searching for and make suggestions for you to select from.

4. Watch as you type; Google is pulling up possible answers to your search before you have even finished. Tap Enter.

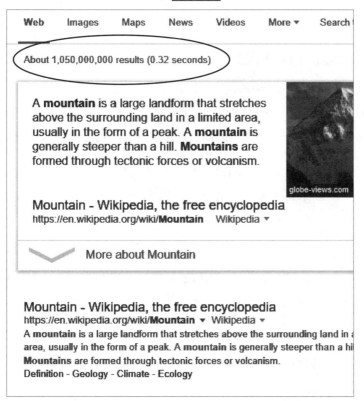

If you don't put enough information into your search, you won't end up with the information you are looking for. The word Mountain *is not specific enough to get you the information you want. Notice the number of pages found at the top of the search results. (The number of results found on your computer may differ.)*

Narrow the Search

Rather than tediously going through search result pages until you see if you can find one about Mount Baker, add some keywords to narrow the search.

5. In the Search box, type **baker** and **skiing** after *mountain*, and then tap Enter.

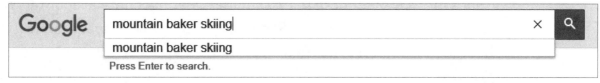

You will notice that by adding just a couple more search terms that the top hits are related to the subject you are looking for. The blue text is the actual link and the title of the page, and the green text is the address of where that page is on the web.

6. Click the **Mt. Baker Ski Area :: Home** link.

   This will take you to the actual website where information about skiing at Mount Baker can be found.

7. Close **Edge**.

. . . .

Improving Your Search Results

Modern searching is pretty straightforward. Search engines are now smart enough that they can usually tell what you are searching for and display the correct search results, but keep the following points in mind to help ensure this is the case:

- **Word order matters:** The first few words in your search should be the main descriptive words for what you are looking for. Other words in your search support these first few words.

- **Type in lowercase:** Always search using lowercase text. If you capitalize words, search engines only look for web pages where words are capitalized. If you don't capitalize, it will look for words of either case.

- **Spelling counts!** If you spell search words wrong, it will search for those wrongly spelled words. Amazingly you will still find results, just not the results you were expecting.

- **Use a minus sign:** If you put a minus sign before a word, the search engine will not show any page that has that word in it. For example, if I am searching for pages on Mount Baker and all I see is pages on skiing, I could use *–skiing* to remove all those ski pages.

Warning! Careful! The minus sign is a clumsy tool. You could end up removing pages with the information you need just because they also reference that particular word you want removed.

- **Type a question:** Modern search engines can understand when you type your search as a complete sentence. Sometimes typing a complete sentence is easier than coming up with primary words.

The World of Search Engines

In this chapter, Google is used to illustrate navigation and search concepts, but it is just one of the many search engines you can use. The web has millions of pages stored on millions of connected computers scattered across the globe, so no single search engine will always provide the information that you're looking for.

Because of the way search engines filter the information shown, you can get different results from using the same search words on different search engines. It is like different chefs cooking the same recipe; each has a "secret ingredient" that gives his or her results a distinct flavor.

Besides Google (www.google.com), other popular search engines include Yahoo! (www.yahoo.com), Bing from Microsoft (www.bing.com), and Ask (www.ask.com).

Many search engines also have specialized searches for specific types of information. Google, for example, has the ability to search just images or just news-related websites.

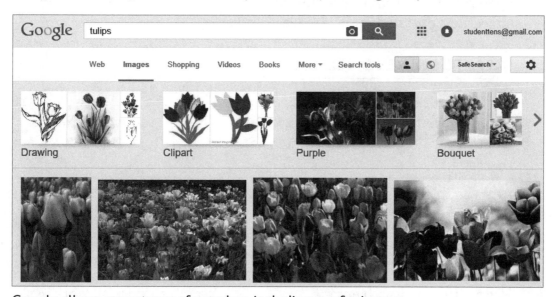

Google allows many types of searches, including one for images.

Despite all of the capabilities these search engines have to index the web, some information is still not within their reach. Many sites that generate their own content (such as newspapers, magazines, and archive sites) do not allow outside search engines to index their sites. They use search engines built into their websites that are designed specifically to search their data. To access the data from this type of site, you would need to go directly to one. This is helpful to know if you're not finding the information you seek with search engines.

The Hidden Web

Only a small fraction of the Internet is indexed by search engines. Much of what is on the Internet is hidden away and needs to be found by other methods. These hidden sites usually require registration and/or payment to use. For example, many schools subscribe to ProQuest, which is a database of research papers and articles perfect for researching information for your own papers. ProQuest is Internet based but not searchable from a search engine.

Luckily your school's library has likely already purchased access to many of these databases of information on the Internet.

Difficult Searches

Most searches are fairly easy. Search engines have gotten powerful enough to interpret your search needs from just a few entered words. However, you will occasionally run into a search that just won't work.

When you're having trouble finding the information you need, consider the suggestions outlined in the following table:

STEPS TO SOLVING A DIFFICULT SEARCH

Try...	Reason...
Put in two or three words that describe what you are looking for (spelled correctly!).	The first few words are the primary triggers for the search engine.
Add a couple more words to narrow the search.	More descriptive words give the search engine more to work with.
Change the word order of your search.	Different primary words will produce a different search result.
Use a different search engine.	Search engines all work in slightly different ways. Using a different search engine may produce a different result.
Search a news, reference, or research site.	Not all information is scanned by search engines. Many sites want you to come and visit them "in person."
Ask a librarian.	Many libraries have a reference librarian who is an expert searcher. They can help you with a difficult search.

Tip! Libraries are no longer just about books. Librarians are gatekeepers and expert resources on information available on the Internet.

Searching for Images

Many search engines, including Google, allow you to search specifically for images. This can be useful, say, when you need images for your research papers and projects.

Tip! Just because a search engine shows you an image, doesn't always mean you have the right to use the image. Copyright laws apply to objects you find while searching. Do your own research regarding copyright laws, and be aware that following them is your responsibility.

HANDS-ON 9.2 Do a Google Image Search

In this exercise, you will use Google to find images of the Grand Canyon.

1. Open **Edge** and go to **google.com**.

2. Type **grand canyon** in the Search box and press [Enter].

3. Click **Images** at the top of the search list.

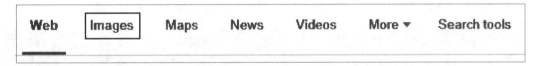

4. Scroll through the images. Note the variety, as well as how the images are sorted by subject at the top of the page.

5. In the search box, add the word **lightning** to the end of your search and press [Enter].

Adding a third search word to your image search narrows the search down to just pictures with lightning in them.

6. Click the first picture.

Notice that when you click the picture you get related images, a link to visit the page that hosts the picture, and a link for viewing the image at its original size. Because images are being added to the Internet daily, the images in your search may be slightly different from those shown here.

7. Close **Edge**.

. . . .

Creating Web Notes in Edge

With Edge, you can take and save notes right on the web pages you are visiting. These notes can take the form of highlights, typed notes, and doodles.

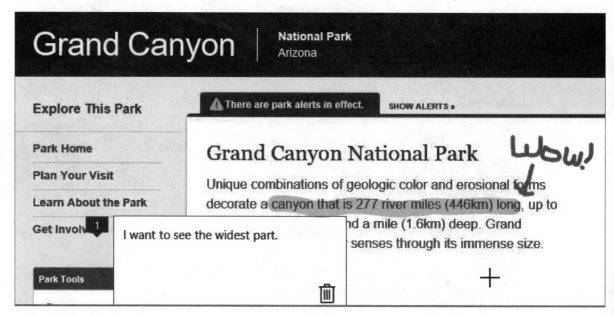

Web Notes can be created by using your mouse, keyboard, or touchscreen (if your laptop has one). Web Notes are a great way to take notes while doing research on the Internet without copying information to a separate program or handwriting it on a piece of paper.

Even better, Web Notes can be shared. You can send Web Notes to someone via email, OneNote (Microsoft's note-taking program), and other programs, depending on what programs are installed on your computer.

Web Notes Tools

Web Notes has various tools for making notes on a webpage.

Highlighter—Use with a mouse or touchscreen to highlight objects on a web page.

Typed Note—Add a typed note to a web page.

Pen—Used to write freehand notes on a web page with the mouse or touchscreen.

Clip—Select the area of the web page to save.

Eraser—Remove notes from a web page.

HANDS-ON 9.3 Make Notes on a Web Page

In this exercise, we will use some of the note tools to mark up a web page.

1. Go to **nps.gov/grca/index.htm**.

2. Click the **Maximize** ☐ button.
   It's easier to make Web Notes when the browser is maximized.

3. Click the **Make a Web Note** ☑ button on the right side of the menu bar.
   Notice that the menu bar changes to show new commands.

4. Click the **Highlighter** 🖊 button.

5. Drag over the facts about how long and wide the Grand Canyon is.

> ## Grand Canyon National Park
>
> Unique combinations of geologic color and erosional forms decorate a canyon that is 277 river miles (446km) long, up to 18 miles (29km) wide, and a mile (1.6km) deep. Grand Canyon overwhelms our senses through its immense size.

6. Click the **Add a Typed Note** 💬 button.

7. Click in the **Grand Canyon** picture at the top of the screen and type **Need to find a picture like this for research paper.**

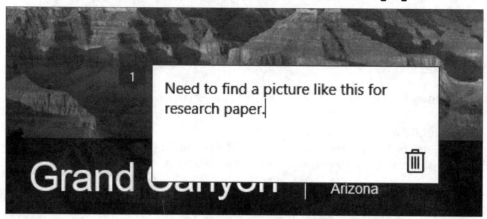

Leave the browser and web page open for the next exercise.

Saving Web Notes

Web Notes can be saved to your Favorites, Reading List, or OneNote. When you save your notes, you are saving a copy of the web page with your notes at the time they were made. The web page may be changed later by its owner, but your copy will remain the same.

HANDS-ON 9.4 **Save a Web Note**

In this exercise, you will save a Web Note.

1. Click the **Save Web Note** 🖫 button on the right side of the menu bar.

2. Click the **Favorites** tab and, if necessary, select **Favorites** from the Create In drop-down menu.

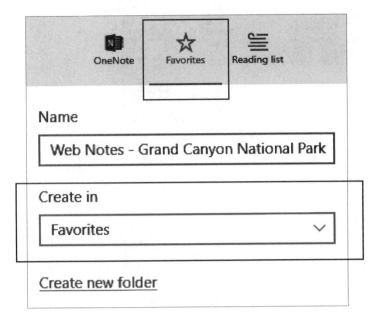

Notice that the names of Web Notes files start with the text Web Notes *so you can tell them apart from other favorites.*

3. Click the **Add** button.

4. Click **Exit** in the top right-hand corner of the Web Notes bar.

5. Click the **Hub** ═ button and then click your **Web Notes – Grand Canyon National Park** favorite.

6. Close **Edge**.

Sharing Web Notes and Web Pages

Edge enables you to share both the Web Notes you create and the web pages you find while searching.

When you are on a page or note, clicking the Share button will bring up various options for sharing. These options will vary depending on what apps are installed on your computer and what services you are signed up for on the Internet.

Defending Yourself from Web Threats

The World Wide Web is a powerful tool that gives you access to information and products. Unfortunately, it also can allow threats, such as computer **viruses**, to access your computer. Once your computer is connected to the Internet, you need to be aware of the threats to it and how to protect against them.

Threats While Surfing

The browser and web pages can be a source of threats to your computer. Web pages can track information using small pieces of code called **cookies**. Not all cookies are bad, but tracking does allow information on you to be kept.

Other websites will try to get you to click on links that will download programs to your computer. This software will run in the background and try to steal passwords, access credit card information, and more.

Advertising on some sites will try to convince you that your machine needs to be fixed or updated and attempt to get you to sign-up for expensive services you don't need.

Protection Software

The first line of protection for your computer is software that monitors and repels or fixes the damage done by various web threats. With the proper software installed on your computer, you will have very few problems when surfing the Internet.

Firewall Software

Firewall software is one way to protect your computer from various Internet threats. A firewall acts much like the outer defensive wall on a medieval castle.

1 Your computer

2 Your firewall

3 The Internet

Windows comes with a built-in firewall. The firewall checks all data coming into the computer and blocks any data (based on rules programmed into the firewall) that is deemed a threat. Many retail firewalls provide additional features like automatic updates, automatic scanning for viruses, and email scanning. Many Firewall programs come in a suite that also includes antivirus and other software designed to protect your computer.

Antivirus Software

Computer viruses are small programs designed to disrupt your computer. They can be picked up from websites, email, and various types of documents. Some viruses are irritating, others destroy files, and the worst try to steal personal information.

Antivirus software works by looking for signs (or "signatures") of viruses in all data coming into the computer and in any files being used by the computer. Some antivirus software also watches the computer for strange activity that may be a sign of a virus infection.

Using Social Media Sites Safely

Social media sites are websites where people and/or businesses with mutual interests are linked in order to communicate. Communications can take many forms: written posts, game play, picture and video sharing, news sharing, and online discussions. Visitors to a site are often encouraged to share comments or join in discussions about information posted. Social sites encourage and facilitate two-way communication.

Social media sites facilitate two-way communication in many ways.

A social media site may have a narrow or a broad focus. YouTube is a site primarily used to share videos. Two popular sites, Facebook and Pinterest, are primarily social networking sites, but they also facilitate picture, video, and music sharing. Blogger provides personal and business blogs for sharing written posts that can include pictures, videos, comments, and discussions. Sites like LinkedIn specifically target businesses, whereas Yelp! targets people who want to share recommendations for services like restaurants.

With any Internet activity, you have to protect your privacy and be vigilant about avoiding scams and the inappropriate use of your personal information. As you link yourself with others online, keep the following information in mind:

- Assume that any information you share on the Internet may stay there *forever*. You must be careful about what you say and be very selective with the pictures and videos you post. The information you post can resurface many years later, and you never know who will see it. The information could become personally embarrassing or adversely affect things like job opportunities.

- Never share your login and password information with anyone.

- Always be wary of "friends" you make online. Your trust should be given carefully to online friends. Scams can happen when online contacts become your friends to gather personal information. Others may take advantage of your network to spread misinformation.

Antispyware

Spyware usually takes the form of cookies and other bits of software that get installed when you visit a website. These bits can gather and store information and be sent to the host, who can then sell your information. Antispyware scans your machine and removes these cookies and software bits, reducing the threat they pose.

Updating Your Software

Most new computers come with antivirus software installed as a free trial, but at some point you will need to pay for a subscription that keeps it updated. Antivirus software needs to be updated regularly, because new viruses are constantly being created. Without updates, your antivirus software will slowly become less effective.

Steps You Can Take

Antivirus and antispyware software will do much of the heavy lifting when it comes to protecting you against web threats, but there are a few simple things you can do to minimize web threats even more and make your Internet experiences safer and a lot more fun!

SAFETY STEPS

Action	Reason
Keep software updated.	Manufacturers update software frequently to fix problems that might cause security issues.
Change passwords frequently.	This makes any passwords that have been exposed on the Internet useless.
Reboot your computer or device every few days.	We tend to leave our PCs and devices on for days and weeks. Rebooting clears any malicious code from memory.
Be aware.	Use the Internet with a bit of caution. Be cautious of untrusted sites, sites with lots of ads, and strange promises.

Concepts Review

To check your knowledge of the key concepts introduced in this chapter, complete the Concepts Review quiz on this page. Or, you can take the quiz online by going to **labyrinthelab/wtcb10**.

Page number

1. Search engines index the web.   true   false   _____

2. Google indexes everything on the Internet.   true   false   _____

3. Search engines search for text only.   true   false   _____

4. Web Notes can be shared multiple ways depending on the apps   true   false   _____
   installed on your PC.

5. Once antivirus software is installed, your computer is protected   true   false   _____
   from most threats—if updated regularly.

6. Passwords should never be changed as it is hard to remember   true   false   _____
   new ones.

7. Which IS NOT a tool found in Web Notes?

   a. Pen

   b. Highlighter

   c. Eraser

   d. Recorder

   Page number: _____

8. Which IS NOT a piece of protection software for your computer?

   a. firewall

   b. antivirus

   c. antispyware

   d. eFence

   Page number: _____

9. When using a search engine, it's best to enter _____.

   a. dozens of words describing what you are looking for

   b. words to vaguely describe what you're looking for to make sure you cover all potential search areas

   c. one word to describe what you're looking for

   d. a few keywords to describe what you're looking for

   Page number: _____

10. Which statement IS NOT true?

    a. Passwords should be changed frequently.

    b. Images and comments posted online eventually get deleted.

    c. Never share your login and password with anyone online.

    d. Antivirus software needs to be updated on a regular basis to stay effective.

    Page number: _____

⚙ Skill Builders

Search for Copyright-Safe Images

Google enables you to search for images that have copyrights that allow for reuse. (You are still responsible for ensuring that images you use for certain purposes are copyright free or in the public domain.) In this exercise, you will use a Google Images search to find a copyright-safe image of the Grand Tetons.

1. Start **Edge** browser and go to **google.com**.

2. In the search box, type **tetons** and press ⌷Enter⌷.

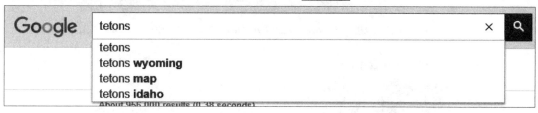

Notice that as you type, Google immediately starts showing relevant information.

3. Click **Images** at the top of the search page.

4. Click **Search Tools**.

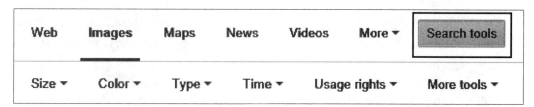

Since we are in Images, the image tools appear (Size, Color, Type, etc.).

5. Click **Usage Rights** and then choose **Labeled for Noncommercial Reuse**.

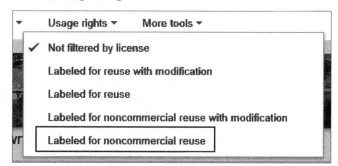

Noncommercial reuse is for use in school papers or any activity that you don't make money from. Notice the screen shows a different collection of images.

SKILL BUILDER 9.2 Save an Image

In this exercise, you will download an image to your computer.

Before You Begin: Make sure your USB flash drive is plugged in.

1. Click any image of the Grand Teton.

Google brings up a bigger version of the image and more options.

2. Click **View Image**.

Google brings up the full-sized image from the site hosting it.

3. Hover over the image with your mouse pointer. If your mouse pointer shows a plus sign, click.

The plus sign means the image is too large for the screen. Clicking shows you the actual size, even if the image is bigger than the screen. Clicking again makes the image fit on the screen.

4. Right-click the image and choose **Save Picture**.

5. Choose your **USB flash drive** and click **Save**.

   A copy of the picture is now saved on your USB flash drive.

6. Click **Back** ← to return to the image search screen.

7. Close **Edge**.

- -

SKILL BUILDER 9.3 Clear Browsing Data

As you use you use the Internet, your browser saves copies of all the information you have viewed. Cookies from the various websites you have visited build up, and the sum total of this information not only becomes a security issue, it slows down the browser. In this exercise, you will clear your browsing data from Edge.

1. Start **Edge**.

2. Click **More Actions** and then choose **Settings**.

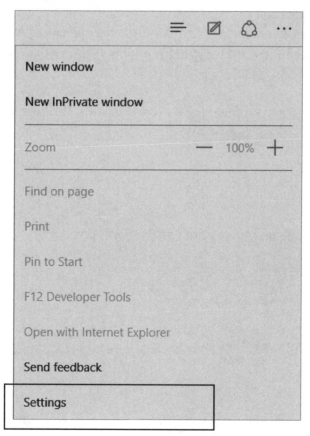

3. Under Clear Browsing Data click **Choose What to Clear**.

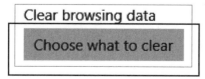

4. Make sure the top three options are selected and then click **Clear**.

The other three items are not as important to clear and might impact your ease of use of the browser if cleared. Clearing data may take a minute as there may be hundreds of small files to delete.

5. While the data is clearing, you will see a Clearing Data… message and a graphic of moving dots at the top of the Settings box.

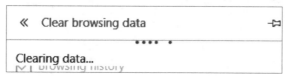

When complete, the message and moving dots graphic will disappear.

SKILL BUILDER 9.4 Search for News

Google enables you to search specifically for news articles on the Internet. In this exercise, you will use Google to search for current news articles on global warming.

1. Start **Edge** and go to **google.com**.

2. Type **global warming** into the search box and press ⏎ **Enter**.

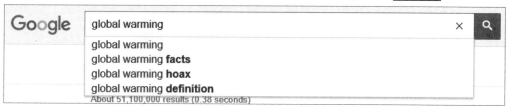

3. Click **News** on the menu bar.

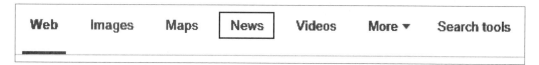

Notice that all the results are now news stories from various news sources.

4. Click **Search Tools**.

Notice that a secondary tool bar appears with tools related to the news.

5. Choose **Sorted by Relevance→Sorted by Date**.

The search results are now sorted by date order with the newest being on top. As you like, take some time to read a few of the articles.

6. Close **Edge**.

CHAPTER 10

Using Settings and Help

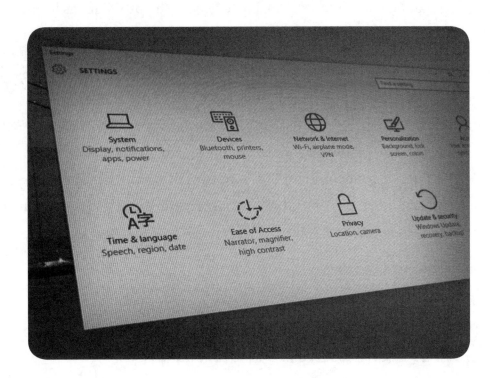

LEARNING OBJECTIVES

- Search your computer using the new Search program
- Use Cortana to talk to your computer
- Change the screen resolution and Desktop background
- Change the power options
- Update Windows 10

Your Windows computer came with a certain look and with the features set to work in a certain way. These settings are not always optimal for the way you like to work. Likewise, it can be difficult to find information and settings on your computer, as Windows has become very complex and has lots of customization options. In this chapter, you will customize the look and feel of your computer and use the new Search feature to search your computer and the Internet for information. You will also update Windows to keep the system and its various features working at their maximum efficiency.

📂 Case Study: Power Options

Dan is frustrated. His new PC laptop is running really slow—even slower than the old laptop that he just replaced. The battery isn't the problem, as he always plugs his laptop into the wall when he is using it.

Dan decides to ask his son Greg, a technologist, about it. Greg has him go into the System command under Settings and look for the Additional Power Settings. Greg tells him that most new PCs and laptops have the power setting set to Balanced, which extends battery life but *really* slows down the computer. He explains that changing to High Performance makes your computer a lot faster and should be the setting you use when plugged into the wall.

System
Display, notifications, apps, power

Choose or customize a power plan

A power plan is a collection of hardware and system settings (like display brightness, sleep, etc.) that manages how your computer uses power. Tell me more about power plans

Plans shown on the battery meter ─────────────────────────

○ **Balanced (recommended)**   Change plan settings
   Automatically balances performance with energy consumption on capable hardware.

⦿ High performance   Change plan settings
   Favors performance, but may use more energy.

Show additional plans ─────────────────────────────── ⌄

Dan makes the changes and is amazed by how much faster his computer runs. Now Dan switches between High Performance and Balanced, depending on whether he is plugged into a power source or running on his battery.

Searching Windows and the Web

Windows 10 includes a new Search Everywhere box on the taskbar. Using this search bar, you can scan for items such as files, folders, and apps on your computer and on the web (using the Bing search engine).

Search results are organized into three sections: Best Match, **Settings**, and Web. The following illustration shows the results of a search for *settings*.

The Settings app is the Best Match, meaning it's most likely what you're looking for.

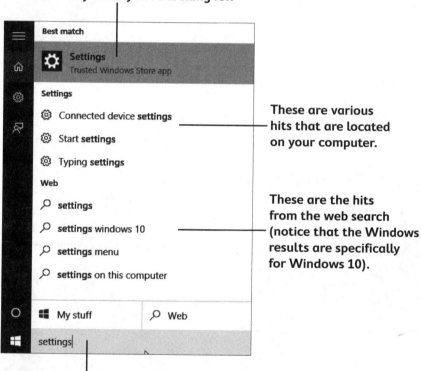

These are various hits that are located on your computer.

These are the hits from the web search (notice that the Windows results are specifically for Windows 10).

Typing "settings" in the Search Everywhere box brings up a variety of hits.

HANDS-ON 10.1 Perform a Basic Search

In this exercise, you will do a basic search using the Search Everywhere box. Before starting the search, you will make sure the Cortana feature is turned off so you can see what a search looks like. The Cortana feature will be explained later in this chapter.

1. Click in the **Search Everywhere** box in the taskbar, to the right of the Start button.

   Ignore any messages that appear.

2. Click the **Settings** button on the left side of the Search pane.

3. Verify that Cortana is turned off. If not, click the slide button to the **Off** position.

4. Click the **Home** button on the left side of the Search pane.

Notice that the search brings up news from the Internet.

5. Click in the **Search Everywhere** box and type `settings`.

Notice that as you type in your search words, the search starts to bring up possible answers.

6. Click **Settings** under Best Match to open the Settings app.

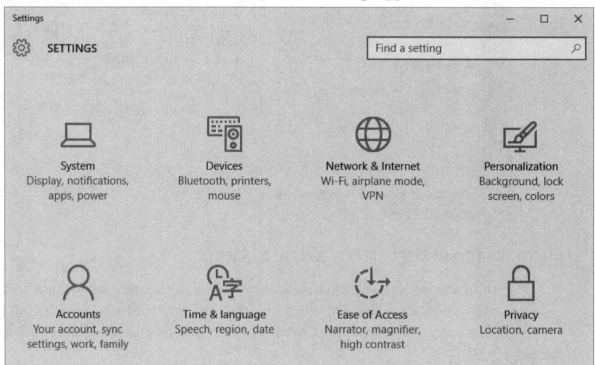

The Settings app is opened.

7. **Close** ⊠ the **Settings** app.

Choosing a Search Link to the Internet

When you select an Internet link from the Search pane, you are actually triggering an additional search using your default browser and the Bing search engine. For example, a search for "research help" brings up several hits under the Web settings. Clicking the "researcher helper" hit opens Edge, and Bing searches for the term. The results may not be what you are looking for, in which case you may need to refine the search using the skills learned in Chapter 9, Researching on the Internet.

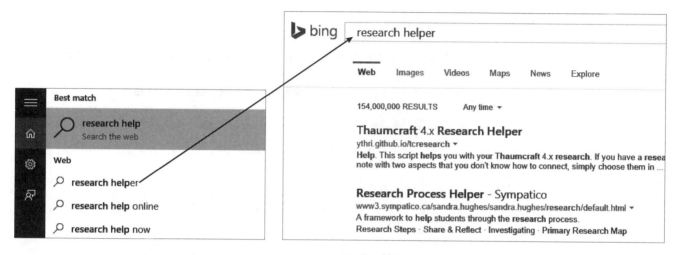

HANDS-ON 10.2 Use Windows to Search the Web

In this exercise, you will use the Search Everywhere box to find help on the web.

1. Click in the **Search Everywhere** box and type `research help`.

   Notice that as you type, Windows Search is already looking for the best answer.

2. Click **Research Help** under Best Match.

   Best Match will show the best result no matter what type of result it is. In this case, it is a web search.

   Watch as your web browser is started and Bing searches the web.

3. Close **Edge**.

Getting Help

The Search Everywhere box can be used to find help for questions you may have about Windows 10. If you are looking for a particular app in your PC, typing the name of it in the Search Everywhere box will usually locate it.

If you need help with a particular app, typing *help with* followed by the name of the app or procedure will usually bring up what you need.

HANDS-ON 10.3 Search for Help

In this exercise, you will use the Search Everywhere box to get help for File Explorer.

1. In the Search Everywhere box, type `help with file explorer`.

2. Under Best Match, click the **Help with File Explorer** link.
    Notice your browser opens to the Bing search engine. The results are based on the text you typed in.

3. In the Bing search box, add `in windows 10` to the end of your search string and tap Enter.
    The search results are now focused on Windows 10.

4. Close **Edge**.

Say "Hey" to Cortana

Cortana is Microsoft's personal digital assistant in Windows 10 and on the Windows Phone, and it will eventually be available on Android and Apple devices. Cortana personalizes your experience with Windows by talking to your computer on your behalf and getting responses back.

Cortana's live tile icon

Cortana not only provides information, she can also start programs and perform simple tasks like reminding you of upcoming appointments. Cortana can be activated by saying, "Hey, Cortana," as she is listening all the time when activated. Keep in mind that Cortana works only on computers and devices with a microphone.

Note! Apple computers and devices, such as iPhones, have a similar personal digital assistant named Siri.

Do I Know You?

▶ View the video "Say 'Hey' to Cortana" on the Student Resource Center at labyrinthelab.com/wtcb10.

Cortana is known by most people in the gaming world. This is because for more than ten years, she has been the digital assistant to Master Chief in the Halo video game series. Cortana was initially just an internal code name for the software, until Microsoft realized that people have a connection to this voice and persona.

In the United States, Microsoft brought back the original voice actress to voice Cortana for Windows 10 and Windows devices.

HANDS-ON 10.4 Set Up Cortana

ON THE WEB In this exercise, you will work within a WebSim to enable and set up Cortana.

1. Launch **Edge** and navigate to the Student Resource Center:
   labyrinthelab.com/wtcb10

2. Click the **Chapter 10** heading to expand the menu, and then click **Hands-On 10.4 Set Up Cortana**.

3. Click in the **Search Everywhere** box on the taskbar and then click the **Settings** button in the left pane.

4. Click the **On/Off** slider to turn Cortana on.

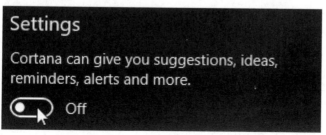

Cortana will now walk you through some setup steps.

5. Click the **I Agree** button to allow Cortana to gather and save information on you.
    This is one of those cases where agreeing to share information is a positive. Cortana works better when you share some information.

6. Type a name you want Cortana to know you by. In this example, type **Anna** and click the **Next** button.

7. Click the **Microphone** button at the end of the search box.

8. Speaking clearly, ask, "What is the weather outside?"

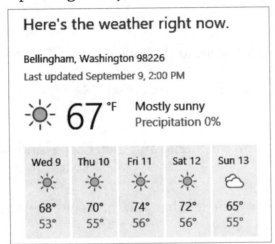

    Cortana will tell you the weather and provide you with a weather report for your location, which for the purposes of this WebSim is Bellingham, WA.

9. Click on the **Desktop** to close the Search box.
    Notice that the Search Everywhere box now shows Ask me anything, *which is your sign that Cortana is turned on.*

10. Click the **Ask Me Anything** box.

11. Click the **Notebook** icon and then click **Settings**.

The Notebook has links to various items Cortana has remembered.

12. Click the **On/Off** slider to turn on the setting that activates Cortana when you say, "Hey, Cortana."

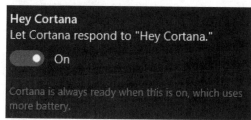

This puts Cortana into listening mode. You can now say, "Hey, Cortana" and not have to click the Microphone button.

13. Say, "Hey, Cortana," pause for a moment, and then say, "Tell me a joke."

Cortana listens for your request and responds with a voice or text answer.

14. Click **Back to Course**.

Talking to Cortana

▶ View the video "Talking to Cortana" on the Student Resource Center at labyrinthelab.com/wtcb10.

Cortana will always respond with at least the results of a web search. With the right command, you can get Cortana to tell you certain information or perform certain tasks. The following table lists some prompts to help you communicate effectively with Cortana.

CORTANA COMMANDS

Command	Cortana...
"Hey, Cortana."	Activates Cortana and makes her listen for your command.
"Tell me a joke."	Tells you a politically correct and safe joke.
"What's the weather outside?"	Tells you the weather for your location and shows the weather forecast.
"Show me directions to..."	Brings up a Bing map of the location.
"Define..."	Tells you the meaning of the given word.
"When is the next [insert team's name] game?"	Brings up that team's game schedule.
"What is...?"	Brings back answers to a definitive question.

There is an amazing range of things Cortana can do. One recent list includes more than 125 commands that Cortana can respond to.

Commands can be spoken or typed into the Search Everywhere box. To find more commands, do a web search for "Windows 10 Cortana commands."

 Tip! Cortana is updated frequently with new commands. Try asking various questions and giving new commands now and then to see what things have been added.

Using Settings

Settings is a very important area in Windows 10. It provides access to most of the programs and features necessary to change the screen appearance and the way things work in Windows.

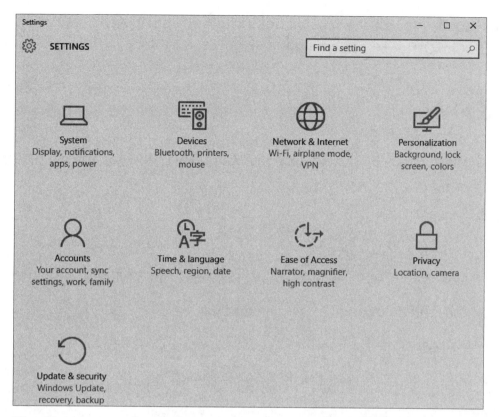

The Settings are divided into nine basic categories. Other categories may be listed as well, depending on your PC, other equipment, and installed software. To access various settings, you can click an item in one of the nine categories or use a keyword search (similar to how you use the Search Everywhere box).

 HANDS-ON 10.5 Change the Time and Date in the Control Panel

 In this exercise, you will use a WebSim to check that the automatic date and time settings are turned on using a category search and a word search in Settings. The Student Resource Center should still be open.

1. If necessary, click the **Chapter 10** heading to expand the menu. Then click **Hands-On 10.5 Change the Time and Date in the Control Panel**.

2. Choose **Start→Settings**.

3. Click the **Time & Language** category.

4. Click **Date & Time** and verify that **Set Time Automatically** is turned on. If not, click the **On/Off** slider to turn it on.

5. Click the back arrow on the top-left corner of the window to return to the main Settings screen.

Search with a Keyword

You can also search for a control via the Find a Setting box in the Settings.

6. Click in the **Find a Setting** box and type `time`.

Notice all the various date and time settings that appear.

7. Click **Date & Time Settings**.

   You are now on the same page where we verified the automatic setting of the time.

8. Click **Back to Course**.

. . . .

Settings vs. the Control Panel

Up until Windows 10, the Control Panel used to contain all the controls that change the way your computer looks and works. Windows 10 uses the Settings app, which gives you an easier layout to work with and makes more of the common controls easier to access.

The Control Panel is still in Windows 10. You will find that Settings switches over to it when you access advanced settings and controls. When Settings accesses the Control Panel, it will bring it up in a separate window.

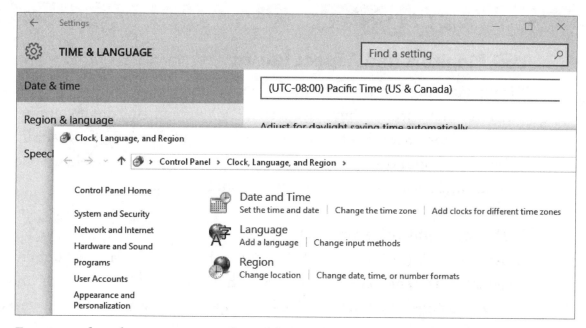

For example, when you access the Additional Date, Time, & Regional Settings area in Settings, you are taken to the Clock, Language, and Region section in the old Control Panel.

Controlling the Screen

One of the many customizations you can make in Windows is to change the resolution of your monitor. Resolution changes the visual appearance of the images on the screen, making objects more or less crisp, or larger or smaller.

Screen Resolution Settings

The digital images you see on your monitor are made up of tiny colored squares called pixels (picture elements). The resolution setting of a monitor establishes how many pixels are displayed horizontally and vertically. A screen setting of 1,024 x 768 pixels is considered low resolution. The pixels are large and may make images have jagged edges. A higher resolution setting like 1,280 x 800 displays more pixels in the same space, so the pixels are smaller. The results are the following:

- Smaller pixels can display finer lines, so images and text look sharper.

- Smaller pixels create smaller images and text, allowing more images and text to fit on the screen.

- Smaller text will be sharper but may be harder to read.

LED Monitors and Aspect Ratios

To take advantage of Windows' marvelous graphics capabilities, people are more often than not opting to buy flat-panel LED (light emitting diode) monitors for their new computers. Because of their trim size and lighter weight, they take up less room on your desktop and are easier to set up and move around than older-style monitors. They are also available in a variety of sizes and shapes.

LED Panels and Wide Screens

Older-style CRT (cathode ray tube) monitors had one screen shape but different diagonal measurements—14-inch, 15-inch, 17-inch, 19-inch, 20-inch, and so on. Newer LED panels vary in both size and shape. The viewable screen is measured diagonally to determine LED size (note that CRT sizing often includes the case).

Different Resolutions, Different Aspect Ratios

LCD screens are assembled with a fixed number of liquid crystals horizontally and vertically (referred to as their native resolution). Although screens have a native resolution, the resolution or number of pixels displayed horizontally and vertically can be changed (see the Changing Monitor Resolution Quick Reference table). Changing the resolution also may change the **aspect ratio** of the screen. If you change to a resolution setting with fewer pixels than the native resolution, the unused screen pixels may appear as black bands above and below the image (letterbox format).

With some resolution settings, monitors may display in letterbox format.

Standard and Widescreen Aspect Ratios

Common aspect ratios for LCD panels

CRT screens (older computer monitors and non-HD TVs) have an aspect ratio of 4:3 (for every four pixels displayed horizontally, three pixels are displayed vertically). LCD screens are available in several aspect ratios, including 4:3.

LCD screens with aspect ratios of 15:9, 16:9, or 16:10 would be called *widescreen*. Keep in mind that when you adjust the screen resolution in Settings, you also may be changing the displayed aspect ratio.

Using the Settings, you can change the screen resolution on most monitors from as low as 800 × 600 to 1,600 × 1,280 or higher.

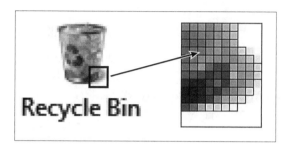

When the Recycle Bin icon is magnified several hundred percent, you can see that is made up of square pixels of different shades and colors.

QUICK REFERENCE: Changing Monitor Resolution

Task	Procedure
Locate the Advanced Display Settings dialog box	■ Choose Start→Settings. ■ From the System category, choose Display. ■ Click Advanced Display Settings (the Resolution box will have the current resolution displayed).
Change the resolution	■ Click the Resolution drop-down menu, choose the desired resolution, and click Apply. ■ The screen may go dark momentarily and then return with the new resolution (if the resolution is higher, items on the screen look smaller, and if the settings are lower, the items look larger). ■ Click Keep Changes to accept or Revert to cancel. ■ If you see a warning saying "Resolution Setting Not Supported," *do not* click any buttons. Let the program revert to the original resolution and then try a different resolution.

Changing the Background Image

The **background** (also called the wallpaper) of the Desktop can be personalized to show a solid color or your favorite image. Computer manufacturers often place their logos on the background or use a design or color that you don't care for, but it's easy and fun to change the background color or image. If you own a digital camera, you have access to an endless supply of possible images of friends, relatives, pets, or your favorite places.

Tip! Avoid images that are cluttered or comprised of colors that make it difficult to see your Desktop icons.

QUICK REFERENCE: Changing the Desktop Background

Task	Procedure
Change the background	■ Choose Start→Settings.
	■ From the Personalization category, choose Background.
	■ Click the Background drop-down menu button and choose Picture, Solid Color, or Slideshow.
	■ Picture: Choose from the menu of recent images or click Browse to search your PC. Then, pick an option from the Choose a Fit menu.
	■ Solid Color: Select an option from the menu of colors.
	■ Slideshow: Click Browse to choose the images to include in the slideshow. Also choose options to set the slideshow time and fit.

Note! In Try This at Home 10.1, you will change the Desktop background on your computer.

Power Options

▶ View the video "Power Options" on the Student Resource Center at labyrinthelab.com/wtcb10.

Power is life when using a laptop or device. With a few preference changes, you can dramatically extend the length of time your laptop can run on batteries. Unfortunately, many of these preferences also slow down your computer or degrade your user experience slightly, so take care when using them.

When your computer is plugged into an outlet, you want to maximize the speed of the system over saving battery power. And when using battery power, you want that power to last as long as possible.

Battery Saver

The Battery Saver setting activates when your battery goes below a 20% charge. Note that Battery Saver makes various changes to your laptop and software, including:

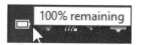

When you hover your mouse pointer over the battery symbol in the system tray, it tells you how much battery life you have left and whether the battery is charging or not.

- slowing the speed at which your processor, hard drive, and other hardware work

- dimming the screen (a bright screen takes more power)

- limiting the activity of background apps, which keeps programs from updating and receiving data (for example, your email app doesn't keep checking for mail unless it is the active app)

You can adjust the settings of the Battery Saver to set when it activates, what programs can continue to run in the background, and more.

Power & Sleep

When Windows detects inactivity, it can turn off the screen after a set amount of time has passed. The screen reactivates after Windows detects a keystroke or mouse movement. This can save a lot of power if you walk away from your laptop to do something else.

You can also set when the laptop goes to sleep. Sleep mode reduces all hardware to a minimal power state, turns off the monitor, and stops all app processes. In this mode, your laptop has the longest battery life possible. When a keystroke is detected or the mouse is moved, the laptop "wakes up" from Sleep. It can take your laptop 30 seconds or more to come out of Sleep mode.

Tip! Some laptops have a problem coming out of Sleep mode, depending on the hardware and software installed. If your laptop never seems to "wake up," you may want to turn this feature off.

HANDS-ON 10.6 Change Power & Sleep Options

 In this exercise, you will work within a WebSim to set the power and sleep options of a typical laptop. The Student Resource Center should still be open in your web browser.

1. If necessary, click the **Chapter 10** heading to expand the menu. Then click **Hands-On 10.6 Change Power & Sleep Options**.

2. Choose **Start→Settings→System**.

3. Click **Power & Sleep**.

Notice that there are two settings for both Screen and Sleep; one for running on battery power and one for when you are plugged in.

4. Under Screen, click the drop-down menu button for battery power and choose **5 Minutes**.

Screen

On battery power, turn off after

| 5 minutes | ⌄ |

After five minutes of inactivity, the screen will turn off.

5. Under Sleep, click the drop-down menu button for battery power and choose **10 Minutes**.

Sleep

On battery power, PC goes to sleep after

| 10 minutes | ⌄ |

After 10 minutes the laptop will go into Sleep mode.

6. Under Screen, set the time to turn off the system when it's plugged in to **10 Minutes**.

7. Choose to **Never** put the PC to sleep when it is plugged in.

   When plugged in, there's no real need to put the laptop to sleep.

8. Close **Settings**.

9. Click **Back to Course**.

. . . .

Additional Power Settings

Many of the additional power settings available have to do with laptops. With these settings you can control what the Power button does, what happens when you close the lid to your computer, and whether you need to reenter a password when your laptop comes out of Sleep mode.

You can also choose and customize power plans. Power plans let you choose between battery life and performance. By default, your PC will have three plans: Power Saver, which maximizes battery life; Balanced, which balances between battery and performance; and High Performance, which maximizes the speed of your computer.

Note! You should check your power-plan settings, even on a desktop PC. Many desktops come set to Balanced instead of High Performance, which means you are not running at the fastest setting your desktop is capable of.

HANDS-ON 10.7 Change the Power Plan

ON THE WEB In this exercise, you will use a WebSim to change the power plan on a PC. The Student Resource Center should still be open in your web browser.

1. If necessary, click the **Chapter 10** heading to expand the menu. Then click **Hands-On 10.7 Change the Power Plan**.

2. Right-click on the battery symbol in the system tray on the left end of the taskbar.

3. On the menu that appears, choose **Power Options**.

This takes you to the Power Options in Settings, where you can choose from various power plans.

4. Click the drop-down arrow at the end of Show Additional Plans.

Show additional plans ⌄

One of the power plans, usually the High Performance one, is hidden below this drop-down menu.

5. Click the radio button (circle) next to **High Performance**.

Hide additional plans

⦿ High performance
Favors performance, but may use more energy.

Your computer is now set to run at its maximum performance.

6. Close **Power Options**.

7. Click **Back to Course**.

Windows Update

Windows is a complex operating system with many components. From time to time, protection against security threats, corrections to errors in the programming, or new features and improvements will be made available as updates. Windows checks for updates roughly once per day. It will also check for updates for other Microsoft products installed on the PC if that option is selected. Your PC automatically installs updates and reboots, if needed. The automatic reboot can be set to a manual reboot in the Settings.

 HANDS-ON 10.8 Setting Update Options

In this exercise, you will set the options for Windows Update. The Student Resource Center should still be open in your web browser.

1. If necessary, click the **Chapter 10** heading to expand the menu. Then click **Hands-On 10.8 Set Update Options**.

2. Choose **Start→Settings→Update & Security**.

3. Click **Windows Update** and then **Advanced Options.**

> ## Windows Update
>
> Your device is up to date. Last checked: Today, 11:45 AM
>
> Check for updates
>
> Available updates will be downloaded and installed automatically.
>
> Advanced options

4. Click the menu button for **Choose How Updates Are Installed** and choose **Automatic**.

5. If necessary, click to add a checkmark in the box next to **Give Me Updates for Other Microsoft Products….**

> Give me updates for other Microsoft products when I update Windows.

6. Click **View Your Update History**.

> ## Update history
>
> Security Update for Microsoft Visual C++ 2008 Service Pack 1 Redistributable Package (KB2538243)
>
> Successfully installed on 9/9/2015
>
> Definition Update for Windows Defender - KB2267602 (Definition 1.205.1823.0)
>
> Successfully installed on 9/7/2015
>
> Definition Update for Windows Defender - KB2267602 (Definition 1.205.1732.0)
>
> Successfully installed on 9/6/2015

This enables you to see the updates that have been installed and remove them if necessary.

7. Close **Settings**.

8. Click **Back to Course.**

The Trend Toward Automatic Updates

As software has become more complicated, automatic updates have become a common software feature. At the same time, more people have access to the Internet (especially high-speed Internet), which makes it easier for developers to send updates electronically.

Before the web, people rarely got updates for their software. They often had to live with any flaws or problems in the software until the next version was available for sale. On occasion, when a flaw was bad enough to make the software unusable, a company might mail registered users a floppy disk with corrections or a corrected version of the program. This happened very rarely, because it was very expensive for the companies, but the web has changed that.

Companies now can post updates on their websites or, better yet, provide automatic updating built into their programs. When automatic updating detects an Internet connection, a program can "call home" and check for updates that add new or improved features, or patches to fix problems. These update files are then automatically transferred to your computer. They either will be automatically installed, or you will be prompted to install them.

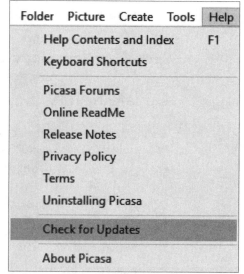

Although automatic updates can be convenient, they can also be annoying when they interrupt you too often while you are trying to work. Programs with automatic update procedures may enable you to set how frequently and at what time of the day they look for updates. You may also be given choices regarding how automatic or manual the process will be.

Many programs that do not have automatic updates allow you to manually check for them. This is generally done by looking for the update command on the Help menu.

The Store

The Store enables you to download apps to your Windows 10 computer in much the same way as you download apps to your phone. This simplifies the process of purchasing and installing new software.

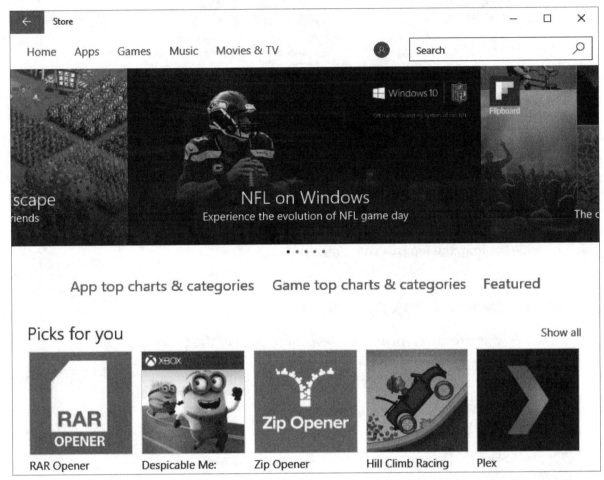

Many of the apps in the Store have a simplified look and feel that works well across Windows PCs, devices, and phones. These apps are also designed to work with touchscreens.

The Store can be opened in two ways: by clicking the Store button on the taskbar and from the All Apps list on the Start menu.

What's in the Store?

The Store has thousands of apps to choose from, and more are being added every week. Apps are currently broken down into four main groups: Apps, Games, Music, and Movies & TV. These groups are then broken down into dozens of categories.

Browse apps

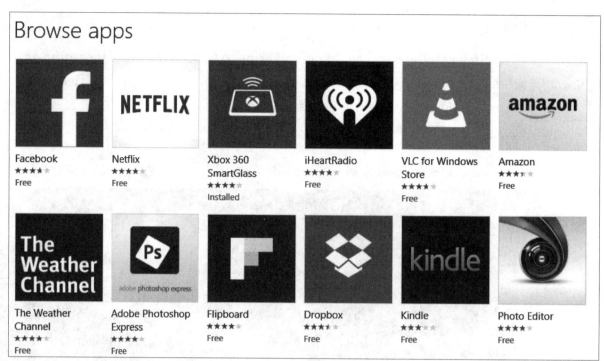

Apps from the Top Free category

HANDS-ON 10.9 Look at Apps

In this exercise, you will review some apps in the Store.

1. Click the **Store** button on the taskbar bar or choose **Start→All Apps→Store**.

2. Click **Apps** from the menu bar.

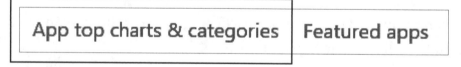

3. In the middle of the page, click **App Top Charts & Categories**.

App top charts & categories	Featured apps

You are now looking at the top free apps.

4. Scroll through the various apps and look for names you recognize. When finished, close the **Store**.

    The stars under the names rate the program on a 1–5 scale that is based on user feedback.

Downloading Apps

Once you have found the specific apps you would like, you will click the Free or Purchase button to download. Because you are in the Store, downloading and installing of the app is all done automatically, so you can continue working on other things and be notified when the app is installed.

HANDS-ON 10.10 Downloading The Weather Channel App

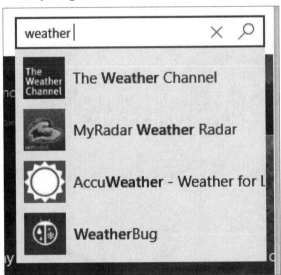

In this exercise, you will download the free Weather Channel app. The Student Resource Center should still be open in your web browser.

1. If necessary, click the **Chapter 10** heading to expand the menu. Then choose **Hands-On 10.10 Download the Weather Channel**.

2. Open the **Store**.

3. In the Search box at the top-right corner of the page, type **weather channel**. When it appears, click **The Weather Channel** from the menu (it usually appears after you get to the end of the word *weather*).

4. On the app's page, click the **Free** button.

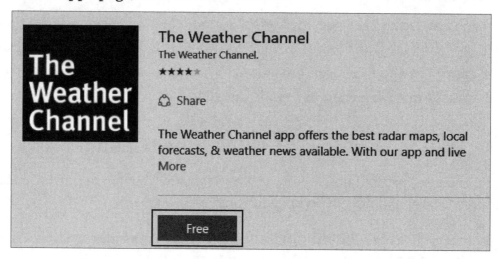

5. Watch as The Weather Channel app starts to download and install. When it's finished, close the **Store**.

6. Choose **Start→All Apps**, and under the "W" apps, click **The Weather Channel**.

7. Close **The Weather Channel** app.

Concepts Review

To check your knowledge of the key concepts introduced in this chapter, complete the Concepts Review quiz on this page. Or, you can take the quiz online by going to **labyrinthelab/wtcb10**.

Page number

1. The Search Everywhere box searches items on your computer only.   **true   false**   _____

2. You can use the Search Everywhere box to get help with Windows 10.   **true   false**   _____

3. You can say "Yo, Cortana" to activate your personal digital assistant.   **true   false**   _____

4. The Control Panel has been completely removed from Windows 10.   **true   false**   _____

5. Increasing the monitor's resolution makes small text sharper but also harder to read.   **true   false**   _____

6. Windows automatically checks for updates.   **true   false**   _____

7. Which of the following are commands you can say to Cortana?

   a. Show me directions to....

   b. Define [insert word].

   c. Tell me a joke.

   d. All of the above

   Page number: _____

8. Increasing the monitor resolution _____.

   a. displays more pixels in the same amount of space on the screen

   b. makes images and text look sharper

   c. allows more images and text to fit on screen

   d. All of the above

   Page number: _____

9. Which IS NOT a default power plan in Windows?

   a. Power Saver

   b. Normal

   c. Balanced

   d. High Performance

   Page number: _____

10. Which statement IS NOT true about Windows Update?

    a. It checks for updates roughly once a day.

    b. Updates are installed automatically.

    c. Reboots must be done manually.

    d. It can check for updates on other installed Microsoft software.

    Page number: _____

Skill Builders

SKILL BUILDER 10.1 Change the Screen Resolution

ON THE WEB In this exercise, you will work within a WebSim to change the resolution of your PC screen.

1. Launch **Edge** and navigate to the Student Resource Center: **labyrinthelabw.com/wtcb10**

2. Click the **Chapter 10** heading to expand the menu and then click **Skill Builder 10.1 Change the Screen Resolution**.

3. Choose **Start→Settings→System**.

4. Click **Display** and then click the **Advanced Display Settings** link.

5. From the **Resolution** drop-down menu, choose **1024 x 768**.

This lower resolution is going to make items on your screen larger, but they won't be as sharp and clear.

6. Click **Apply**.

Notice that the screen changes to the new resolution.

7. Ignore the message (don't click either option) and let the screen revert back to its starting resolution.

Keep these display settings?

Reverting to previous display settings in 11 seconds.

Keep changes   Revert

8. Change the resolution to **800 x 600**.

   Notice how large everything is on the screen.

9. Let the screen revert to its starting resolution.

10. Close **Settings**.

11. Click **Back to Course**.

SKILL BUILDER 10.2 Search with Cortana

In this exercise, you will use Cortana to find information about the Grand Canyon.

Before You Begin: You will need to be on a machine with a microphone and Cortana activated.

1. Click the **Microphone** button at the end of the **Ask Me Anything** box.

2. Say, "How deep is the Grand Canyon?"

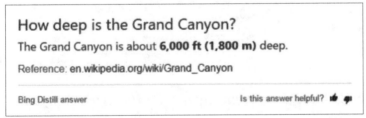

How deep is the Grand Canyon?
The Grand Canyon is about **6,000 ft (1,800 m)** deep.

Reference: en.wikipedia.org/wiki/Grand_Canyon

Bing Distill answer   Is this answer helpful?

Cortana will start your browser and bring up a Bing search with the correct answer on top.

3. Click the **Microphone** button and say, "Show me images of the Grand Canyon."

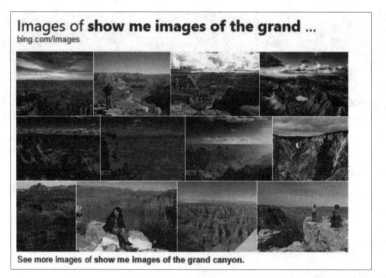

Images of show me images of the grand ...
bing.com/images

See more images of show me images of the grand canyon.

Cortana will bring up a Bing search in your browser containing a list of images to choose from.

4. Click the **Microphone** button and say, "What is the weather like at the Grand Canyon?"

Here's the weather right now.

Grand Canyon
Last updated September 14, 10:00 AM

☀ **78**°F   Mostly sunny
Precipitation 70%

Mon 14	Tue 15	Wed 16	Thu 17	Fri 18
⛅	⛅	☀	☀	☀
83°	85°	84°	85°	87°
66°	66°	59°	61°	60°

Data from Foreca

Cortana will say and show the current weather for the Grand Canyon.

5. Click on the **Desktop** to close the Search box.

6. Close **Edge**.

· ·

Try This at Home

TRY THIS AT HOME 10.1 **Change the Screen Background**

In this exercise, you will add an image to your Desktop background.

1. Choose **Start→Settings**.

2. Click **Personalization** and then **Background**.
   This brings up the Background pane for changes to the look of the background.

3. Click the drop-down button under the Background option and choose **Picture**.

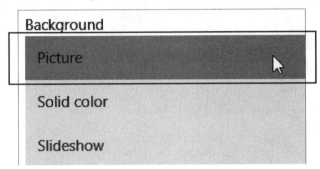

4. Click on a picture from the sample list provided.
   You can use the Browse button to find one of your own images on your PC or USB flash drive. Notice how the image selected is immediately placed on the background screen.

5. Click on the drop-down button under Background and choose **Solid Color**.

6. Select any color.
   Notice how the background immediately changes to that color.

7. Select a **Picture** or **Solid Color** to use as your background.

8. Close **Settings**.

· ·

TRY THIS AT HOME 10.2 **Find and Change the Screen Saver**

In this exercise, you will search settings for the screen saver controls and then enable a screen saver.

1. Choose **Start→Settings**.

2. In the Find a Setting box type `screen saver`.

Search results will appear as you type.

3. Click **Change Screen Saver**.

The screen saver dialog box appears. Notice that it looks different from Settings because it is from the old Control Panel.

4. The Screen Saver Settings may appear underneath the Settings screen. Click the **Screen Saver** title bar to make it the active program and on top.

5. From the drop-down list in the Screen Saver Settings window choose **Mystify**.

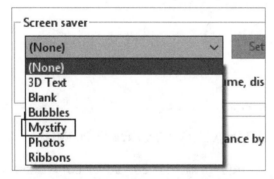

The Preview monitor at the top of the screen should show you what the screen saver looks like. The preview button can also be used to see the screen saver in full screen view.

6. Change the wait time to **5** minutes.

The screen saver will come on after 5 minutes of inactivity.

7. Look through the various screen savers, pick your favorite, and set your preferred wait time.

8. Click **OK**.

9. Close **Settings**.

. . . .

Glossary

active   The app currently in use.

aspect ratio   The relation between width and height on a computer monitor.

background   The image or color covering your Desktop; also called wallpaper.

bandwidth   The amount of data your Internet connection can provide.

browser   A program used to access the web. (*Examples:* Edge, Chrome)

cloud computing   Apps and services that run from the Internet.

cloud storage   File storage on the Internet.

command   Launches a program task.

cookie   Code in a webpage used to track your preferences.

Cortana   A personal digital assistant that enables you to control your computer with voice commands.

cursor   A blinking indicator of where text will appear on the screen when typing. *See also* insertion point

domains   Divides Internet addresses into groups with a common purpose. (*Examples:* .com, .net, .gov)

drag-and-drop method   A way to move screen objects in Windows 10.

drive letter   An alphabetical designation assigned to storage devices. (*Examples:* C:, Removable drive F:)

Favorite   A link you save in your browser.

flip   A method for switching between open apps.

floppy disk   An obsolete removable disk technology.

galleries   Collections of tools or options on a Ribbon.

gesture   A touchscreen control.

hard drive   The permanent storage in your computer.

Hub   The central collection point in Edge for everything you save from the Internet.

hyperlink   A link in a web page that jumps you to another place on the web.

insertion point   A blinking indicator showing where text will appear when typing on a computer. *See also* cursor

Internet service provider   *See* ISP

ISP   Internet service provider; a business that provides access to the Internet.

live tiles   Representations of apps used in place of icons that show updated information from the app.

mouse pointer   The indicator that moves on the screen in response to the movement of the mouse.

network   A collection of computers and devices connected together to share information.

operating system   The software that manages your computer. (*Examples:* Windows 10, Windows 7, Windows XP, Linux, OSX)

path   Shows the location of a file or folder within the organization of a drive.

permanent storage   A device that stores data until erased. (*Examples:* hard drive, USB flash drive)

pinned   Items placed on the Start menu as tiles for easy access; can be organized per the user's preference.

Quick Access toolbar   A small toolbar containing common commands.

Ribbon   A program feature used to display program commands instead of using traditional menus and toolbars.

router   A device that enables multiple computers to connect to the Internet.

search engine   A specialized page used to find information on the web. (*Examples:* Google.com, Ask.com)

selected   Text that is highlighted and ready to be formatted or changed in some way.

Settings   A Windows 10 app containing all the customization and setup controls.

sleep mode   Computer state in which the computer uses very little electricity and has little activity.

social media site   Web pages where people and businesses are linked to discuss mutual interests.

spyware   A program designed to secretly gather information from your computer.

subfolder   A folder within a folder.

Uniform Resource Locator   See URL

URL   Uniform Resource Locator; address for a resource on the Internet.

viruses   Small programs written to disrupt your computer.

web   Common name for the World Wide Web.

Index

documents
    data file sizes, 168
    printing, 107–109
    saving, 90–93
domains, 223–224
Drag-and-Drop method, using with files and folders,
    194–196
dragging
    with mouse, 12–14
    multiple files, 198
drawing in Paint app, 86–87
drive order, 158
drives, navigating with File Explorer, 163. *See also* hard
    drives; storage drives
drop-down menus, 83–84, 99–100
DVD drives, 155

E

Edge browser, 222. *See also* Hub
    navigation, 225–226
    Web Notes, 256–260
editing text, 103–111
.edu domain, 224
email. *See also* messages; Outlook.com
    attachments, 130–132
    dragging to folders, 137–138
    explained, 121
    folders, 135–136
    moving, 136–137
    safety, 138–143
    saving, 135–138
    sending messages, 125–132
email address
    explained, 122
    saving, 138
Enter key, 102
Eraser tool, 97
Explorer. *See* File Explorer
external hard drives, 156

F

favorites, using in Hub, 232–238
File Explorer. *See also* folders
    address bar, 164–166
    Back and Forward buttons, 166–167
    file and folder layout, 169
    folder contents, 172
    folder window tasks, 162–163
    Folders pane, 172–174
    folders and subfolders, 164
    locating folders, 163
    navigating, 165–166, 174
    sorting feature, 169–171
    subfolders, 173
    View tab, 169–170

File menu, 83
filenames, 89–90
files
    copying and moving, 195–196
    deleting, 199–201
    and folders, 88
    moving and copying, 190–198
    opening, 12
    renaming, 185–186
    restoring, 199–201
    searching for, 175–176
    selecting, 196–198
    storage of, 184–185
    uploading to OneDrive, 205–206
Firefox browser, 222
firewall software, 261
flash drives
    explained, 156
    saving work to, 89, 92
Flip command, 56–58
floppy disk drives, 158
folders. *See also* File Explorer
    creating, 183
    creating on Desktop, 186–187
    creating on USB flash drive, 188–190
    deleting, 199–201
    and files, 88
    locating with File Explorer, 163
    moving and copying, 190–198
    navigating with File Explorer, 163
    opening, 12
    organizing, 192–193
    renaming, 185–186
    restoring, 199–201
    and subfolders, 164
Font group, drop-down lists in, 99–100
formatting text, 105–107
.fr country code, 225

G

galleries, 85, 94–95
gestures. *See* touch gestures
GHz (gigahertz) ratings, explained, 8
gigabyte (GB/gig), measurement of, 168
Google Chrome browser
    described, 222
    searching with, 250–252
Google image search, performing, 255–256
.gov domain, 224

H

hard drives. *See also* drives
    explained, 8
    external, 156
    saving to, 88–91

U

.uk country code, 225
unlocking Windows 10, 16
Update options, setting, 290–292
updating software, 263
URLs (Uniform Resource Locators), 223–225
.us country code, 225
USB (universal serial bus) port, 9
USB flash drives
    creating folders on, 188–190
    explained, 156
    vs. OneDrive file storage, 201
    plugging in and unplugging, 159–161
    saving work to, 89, 92
    viewing, 161
users, switching, 16

V

Victoria Free-Net, 217
video files, data file sizes, 168

W

wallpaper, changing, 286
Weather Channel app, downloading, 295–296
web, navigating, 225–226
web browsers. *See* browsers
Web Notes
    creating in Edge browser, 256–260
    sharing, 259–260

web pages
    making notes on, 257–258
    navigating, 227
    printing, 232–238
    sharing, 259–260
web search. *See* searching
web threats, defending against, 260–263
websites
    Ask search engine, 253
    Bing search engine, 253
    Firefox browser, 222
    Google Chrome browser, 222
    search engines, 253
    top-level domains, 224
wide screens and LED panels, 284
windows. *See also* app windows
    identifying, 7
    moving and resizing, 44–45
    resizing, 43
    snapping, 43–45
Windows 10, logging in to, 5–7
Windows folder, contents of, 184
Windows Update, 290–291
wireless networks and connections, 219, 221
Word
    starting online, 77–78
    typing in, 99–102
work area, 93–98
World Wide Web, 217

Z

zooming, 46